RCIA

Renewing the Church as an Initiating Assembly

RCIA

RENEWING THE CHURCH AS AN INITIATING ASSEMBLY

Lawrence E. Mick

THE LITURGICAL PRESS
COLLEGEVILLE, MINNESOTA

COVER DESIGN: Mary Jo Pauly

Nihil obstat: Daniel J. Taufen, S.T.L., *Censor deputatus.*
Imprimatur: ✛ Jerome Hanus, O.S.B., Bishop of St. Cloud. March 21, 1989.

Library of Congress Cataloging-in-Publication Data
Mick, Lawrence E., 1946–
    RCIA : renewing the Church as an initiating assembly.

    1. Catholic Church.   Ordo initiationis Christianae
adultorum.   2. Initiation rites—Religious aspects—
Catholic Church.   3. Catholic Church—Liturgy.   I. Title.
BX2045.I553M53   1989   264'.020813   89-7988
ISBN 0-8146-1787-5

THIS BOOK IS DEDICATED to all those catechumens and candidates who have shared their faith journey with me over the past fifteen years. Through them I have come to know more deeply the awesome presence and power of God in our lives. I have been constantly called to a deeper conversion in my own life and have found my faith strengthened in the Spirit they have shared.

May God keep them always alive in that Spirit.

CONTENTS

PREFACE

"When I was a child, I used to talk as a child, think as a child, reason as a child; when I became a man, I put aside childish things" (1 Corinthians 13:11). But some things from childhood we keep, and one thing I have kept is a fondness for putting jigsaw puzzles together, especially on quiet, snowy evenings at home.

I remember once as a child trying for a very long time to figure out where a particular piece fit into a puzzle. No matter how I turned it or where I tried it, it just wouldn't fit. It was only when the puzzle was almost completed that I realized that my mystery piece actually belonged to another puzzle! It had somehow escaped from its box and had accidentally been put with the wrong puzzle because it looked as if it belonged there.

From that incident I learned a lesson I have never forgotten: No matter how hard we try, it is not possible to make a piece fit if we're trying to put it into the wrong puzzle. I suspect that this is the problem faced by many people in trying to implement the Rite of Christian Initiation of Adults (RCIA). The natural impulse is to try to fit this new piece into the old puzzle, to simply add the RCIA to the usual activities and programs of the parish or to put the new piece in the place of the former "convert classes." But the piece won't fit. We can force it into the old puzzle, but only if we mangle it or cut part of it off or distort it in some other way.

What we really need is a new puzzle. The RCIA calls us to radical reform and renewal as a Church, and that means that we need a lot of new puzzle pieces. They may fit together as the pieces of the old puzzle did, but it will be a new picture that results. Any attempt to force the RCIA to fit into the old puzzle will only ruin it and will result in a strange-looking picture of a parish.

As Ralph Kiefer noted back in 1974, the new rites of initiation are, "historically and culturally speaking, a massive rejection of the presuppositions both of pastoral practice and of most churchgoers regarding the true meaning of Church membership. This is a revolution quite without precedent, because the Catholic Church has never at any time in its history done such violence to its ritual practice as to make its rites so wholly incongruous with its concrete reality. Such an act is either a statement that rite is wholly irrelevant or a statement that the church is willing to change, and to change radically, that concrete reality. Such an approach is either suicide or prophecy of a very high order" ("Christian Initiation: The State of the Question," in *Made, Not Born* [Univ. of Notre Dame Press, 1976], pp. 149–150). I believe that it is prophecy of a very high order, but some prophecies take a long time to reach fulfillment. The revival of the catechumenate and the accompanying renewal of our initiatory practice will happen slowly and gradually. But I really believe that the effort is worth whatever time and energy it requires, because the RCIA offers the best hope we have of becoming a renewed and vibrant Church, the kind of Church envisioned by the Second Vatican Council and, I believe, the kind of Church that the Lord calls us to be.

For this renewal to be truly fruitful, it is essential that we recognize as clearly as possible the picture on the new puzzle and then examine carefully the different pieces that go together to make up that picture. It is all too easy to slip back into the old puzzle, to miss the implications for change and rethinking that are inherent in the RCIA. We need to be clear about what we are trying to do in the catechumenate itself and then explore the ramifications of that rite for everything else that we do as Church. Those two goals are the purpose of this book.

CHAPTER ONE

THE ORIGINS OF THE RCIA

Those confronting the Rite of Christian Initiation of Adults for the first time might well ask, "How did the Church come up with all this?" It seems to be a far cry from the inquiry classes and private baptism ceremonies that had been customary in most of our parishes. Why such a drastic change? And where did all these rituals and prayers come from?

Most of what is found in the RCIA is actually quite ancient, having been developed in the early centuries of the Church's life. The RCIA is in large part a restoration or recovery of initiation patterns and practices that the Church used in its early days. Therefore it will be valuable to begin our consideration of the RCIA with a brief look at the history of Christian initiation from the New Testament period until our own time.

The New Testament Period

When we turn to the New Testament to learn how initiation was celebrated at the beginning of the Church's life, we find precious little information. Much can be found on the meaning of baptism, but very little on the rite itself or the process of initiation. And what we do find is often unclear and controverted.

In the Acts of the Apostles, for example, we find mention of baptism in the name of the Lord Jesus, while Matthew's Gospel speaks of baptism in the name of the Trinity. Were these two different rituals for baptism? Or was baptism in the name of Jesus—that is, into his death and resurrection—always administered in the name of the Father, Son, and Holy Spirit? The evidence is just not that clear.

St. Paul, in Romans 6:3-11, gives us a rich description of the meaning of baptism, and perhaps he hints at how the rite was celebrated: going down into the pool (tomb) with Christ and rising on the other side. Archeology has provided evidence of such a practice by unearthing baptismal fonts dating some years later and built with three steps leading down into a pool of water. But then one must ask: Was Paul describing what was already being done, or did the early Christians build the baptismal fonts that way after reading Paul?

A couple of things are clear in the New Testament. One is that the water bath of baptism was the means of entrance into the Church community. There was apparently one major exception to this: Nowhere is there any indication that the twelve Apostles were baptized, but for everyone else this rite was required. Perhaps because the Twelve had experienced the death and resurrection of Christ personally, it was not considered necessary for them to experience it ritually.

It is also clear in the New Testament that initiation into the Church was an insertion into the death and resurrection of Christ, which was the point of transformation of the whole of history and thus of the life of the initiate as well. It was initiation into a transformed community of faith, a community that was called by God to be God's people for the sake of the world. Hence, initiation involved a mission of service in the name of the Lord, a call to carry on Christ's redeeming work in the world.

The approach to preparation for baptism is even less clear in the New Testament. We have the story of Philip and the Ethiopian eunuch in Acts 8. After a brief discussion of the good news of Jesus, they came to some water and the eunuch was baptized on the spot. That's hardly a three-year catechumenate! But was this the normal approach to baptism or an extraordinary situation? In any case, it does suggest to us that the catechesis for baptism included reflection on the Old Testament (they began with a discussion of Isaiah) as a basis for understanding the Jesus-event: "Then Philip opened his mouth and, beginning with this scripture passage, he proclaimed Jesus to him" (Acts 8:35).

Some scholars suggest that the household codes found in Paul's letters (for example, Romans 12-13; Ephesians 4:17-6:9; Colossians 3:5-25) may be indications of a very early instruction for catechumens, emphasizing the virtuous life lived in Christ Jesus. But here, as with most of the New Testament evidence on initiation, we can only speculate.

The Early Centuries

As we move beyond the New Testament, we begin to find a few more hints of the shape of preparation for initiation. The *Didache*, dating from the late first/early second century, contains a partial catechism and gives instructions for celebrating baptism. It offers an instruction on the "Two Ways," the Way of Life and the Way of Death, which precedes its discussion of baptism and thus may well have been the focus of the prebaptismal catechesis. The *Didache* also indicates a preference for cold, running water for the celebration of baptism—obviously baptism was a powerful experience in those days!

Justin Martyr (ca. 150 A.D.) says that those who believe the truth of the Christian teaching promise to live according to this doctrine. Then they are taught to pray and seek forgiveness of their sins with fasting, while the community of the faithful fast and pray with them. They are then baptized in the name of the Trinity and are called "the enlightened" and "the purified," because they have been enlightened by the truth and have purified their lives to live the Christian way.

Irenaeus of Lyons (born ca. 140 A.D.) suggests the use of a catechesis based on the history of salvation and a typological use of Scripture, that is, seeing Old Testament figures as "types" fulfilled in Christ. Tertullian (born ca. 160 A.D.) seems to put more emphasis on moral exhortation, asking whether the catechumens can live up to the Christian way of life.

Origen, who headed the great school at Alexandria from 202 to 234 A.D., gives us an important insight into the catechumenate. The school at Alexandria had been started by Bishop Demetrius to present the Christian philosophy of life, in competition with the various philosophical schools in that great city of learning in the ancient world. In this school the Christian gospel was translated into the philosophical terms of the day, and this became the basis for the development of Origen's theology. In the catechumenate the gospel and the culture in a given time and place meet and interact. Translating the gospel within and over against the culture is what is meant by theology. Far from being a watered-down Sunday school class, the catechumenate was the forum in which the gospel and a culture grappled with one another, the place where some of the most profound theology of the time was developed, the context in which the Church thought through the implications of the gospel for the problems and issues of the day. We will do well to remember that insight as we attempt to recover the catechumenate today.

The Golden Age of the Classical Catechumenate

The golden age of the catechumenate extended roughly from the third to the fifth century. In this period it reached its fullest development and its widest use. As we have seen, it did not arise suddenly full-blown but resulted from a process of formalization of what had existed informally from the early days of the Church.

Several historical pressures led to the formalization of the initiation process. The first was the need to reinterpret the Jesus tradition in a variety of new missionary contexts (as in Alexandria). This required much more time and effort at catechesis than when the gospel was spreading among people already familiar with the Old Testament and with the time in which Jesus lived and died and rose again.

The second pressure was the need to standardize Christian teaching and to strengthen the catechesis. This was important in part because of the competition from pagan philosophies, from heretical movements, and from the mystery religions. There was a need for more thoroughness and more consistency in what was being taught, so that new Christians would be well-formed in the Christian beliefs.

The third pressure was the need to probe potential candidates more carefully. The community sought to exercise more control over who was admitted. This was important in order for the community to uphold its standards so that it could give effective witness to the world. A good example of that concern can be found in the *Apostolic Tradition* of Hippolytus, written probably around 215 A.D. in Rome. Hippolytus prescribes a rather rigorous probing of candidates as to their occupation and way of life. The text reads almost like a litany: "If a man is a procurer, that is, supports prostitutes, let him give it up or be sent away. If he is a sculptor or painter, he is to be instructed not to make any more idols. Let him give it up or be sent away." If he is an actor or a charioteer or a wrestler or a gladiator, etc., "let him give it up or be sent away." The Church in those times apparently had little hesitation about refusing those who were not willing or ready to live up to the demands of the Christian way of life. Those who were accepted as catechumens underwent three years of instructions with prayers. Some scholars suggest that Hippolytus was "upping the ante" a bit here and that two years of instruction had been the custom of the time. If that is so, Hippolytus had an impact, for a three-year pattern became common after his time. At the end of the three years, the lives of the catechumens were to be examined, and if the catechumens were found to be ready, they were "elected" or chosen to receive the sacraments, which were celebrated at Easter.

By the fourth century the catechumenate was at its peak, with a fully developed process of formation and a rich variety of ritual actions to celebrate the initiation process. In those days the Church did not have the degree of communication and centralization that are familiar to us, so the process and the rites varied from city to city and region to region. To give a detailed account of these variations is beyond the scope of this book, but we can offer a composite picture of initiation in the fourth century. It would not have taken place exactly this way anywhere, but these patterns were typical of the process.

Admission to the catechumenate was celebrated ritually with the sign of the cross, the giving of salt, an imposition of hands, and sometimes a prayer of exorcism. A three-year process of instruction and formation followed, during which time the catechumens shared in the life of the community by study, prayer, and service. They also joined in the Sunday worship, but were generally dismissed after the liturgy of the Word (long called the Mass of the Catechumens), since only the baptized were allowed to participate in the Eucharist itself.

When it was judged that the catechumens were ready for the sacraments of initiation, they began a period of spiritual preparation leading up to the sacraments at Easter. This is the origin of Lent. This period was often begun with a scrutiny of their lives and prayers of exorcism, followed by an enrollment for baptism. They were expected to attend the daily Lenten liturgy (this was not yet daily Eucharist), to do penance as a discipline, and, in some regions, to confess their sins. Some writers also talk about a prebaptismal bath on Holy

Thursday. This derived from a common penance of not bathing during Lent; they were then urged to bathe on Holy Thursday "lest they dirty the baptismal water too much."

The rites for the Easter Vigil were rich and beautiful. In the West they began with the "opening" of the ears and mouth to hear and speak the word of God. The candidates then faced west to renounce Satan, the lord of darkness, and then faced east to adhere to Christ, the rising Son of God. Then they were anointed with oil as a sign of strength for the struggle with Satan. Next they stripped naked (this was done before the anointing if the whole body was anointed) and may have had a second anointing. The font was then blessed by invoking the Holy Spirit to sanctify the waters. This blessing was generally considered essential and was seen as a parallel to the blessing over the bread and wine at the Eucharist. Baptism was administered by immersion three times in a waist-deep pool. Saint Ambrose notes that in Milan there was a washing of the feet after the baptism, deriving no doubt from the statement of Jesus at the Last Supper, "Whoever has bathed has no need except to have his feet washed . . ." (John 13:10). Coming out of the water, the newly baptized were clothed in white garments, anointed on the forehead (if there was not a second anointing earlier), given a holy kiss, presented with a lighted candle (this is uncertain), and sent into the midst of the assembly of the faithful, who had been listening to readings and praying for those being baptized. Then together they celebrated the Easter Eucharist. The newly baptized were sometimes given milk and honey with the Eucharistic bread and cup as a sign of entering the Promised Land.

We have taken the time to describe these rites at some length to reveal how similar our renewed initiation rites are to this early pattern. There is very little that is new in the Rite of Christian Initiation of Adults. It is a restoration or renewal in the best sense of those terms.

The Disintegration of the Initiation Pattern

Having reached a peak in the fourth century, the Church's process and rituals of initiation fell on hard times soon afterward. There were several dimensions to this disintegration. The rites of initiation became separated over time because of various historical factors. In the classic pattern, what we know as baptism, confirmation, and first Eucharist were all celebrated in the same ceremony at the Easter Vigil as an integrated ritual of initiation. By the fifth century this pattern began to break down as confirmation was detached from the other sacraments. The main reason for this was the growth in the size of dioceses. When the diocese basically consisted of one city, the whole church gathered with the bishop to celebrate initiation at Easter. As dioceses grew and churches multiplied, this became more difficult, and the development of rural dioceses made it impossible.

Since the anointing after baptism had generally been done by the bishop, the question arose of what to do when the bishop was not presiding at the initiation. Two different answers were given. In the East the presiding minister, whether bishop or presbyter (priest), was designated as the proper minister of the postbaptismal anointing (confirmation). Thus the East has maintained, even to the present day, the integrity of initiation, celebrating baptism, confirmation and Eucharist in the same ceremony for all who are initiated into the Church.

In the West this anointing was reserved to the bishop, even though that meant it had to be given after the Easter Vigil ceremony. At first the bishop would just make the rounds during Easter week or the Easter season and "complete" the initiation. But as dioceses grew larger yet and bishops began to take on responsibility for civil government after the fall of the Roman Empire, confirmation got delayed longer and longer. As the centuries passed, the gap between the initiation rites widened more and more. Local synods and councils called for parents to bring their children (it was mostly children who were baptized by this time) for confirmation before their first birthday. Later they specified at least by their third birthday, then their fifth, etc., until eventually confirmation came to be regularly celebrated at age fourteen.

Knowing the history of this disintegration does not explain how such a process could have been allowed to occur. Nathan Mitchell has offered some insight into the dynamics that underlay this separation of baptism and confirmation (see "Dissolution of the Rite of Christian Initiation," in *Made, Not Born* [Univ. of Notre Dame Press, 1976]). Mitchell suggests several factors that worked together to undermine the unity of the initiation ritual. The first he calls the problem of accumulated symbolism. Over a period of time the central symbols of the sacraments tend to attract a variety of lesser symbols that embellish the rite. Examples of this in baptism would include the clothing with a white garment, the lighting of a baptismal candle, and the rite of opening the ears and mouth (Ephphetha). Such symbols are an enrichment of the celebration unless they get out of hand. If too many symbols become clustered around a given rite, people can begin to lose sight of what is central and what is peripheral, especially if there is a decline in adequate catechesis. This process is evident in the case of initiation. Both the water bath and the anointing gathered a variety of secondary symbols around them, to the extent that the original connection between these two central symbols was forgotten.

The second factor noted by Mitchell was the loss of symbolic intelligibility. Symbols "speak" to us on many different levels at once, suggesting a whole range of associations and insights, and affecting us emotionally and psychically as well as intellectually. The meaning of these symbols can be lost, however, if they are separated too far from our normal human experience, or if the symbols are used so minimally that their richness is lost. Both of these things happened to our liturgy in the Middle Ages: the worship of the Church became increasingly separated from the daily life of the people and the focus on questions of validity of the sacraments led to a minimal use of the sacramental symbols, such as using just a few drops of water, a smudge of oil, etc.

With this minimalism we lost the full power of the symbols to involve several of our senses and thus draw us deeply into the experience of the ritual. Nowhere is this more evident than in the shift from baptism by immersion to our experience of baptism as a trickle of water over the forehead. We can still speak of water as a sign of death and life, since water can kill by drowning and yet nothing can live without it. But even if we know that in our heads, we come to *know* it at deeper levels of our being if we are immersed three times under the water and experience both the threat of drowning and the exhilaration of rising from the watery tomb to newness of life.

Mitchell's final suggestion is that the Church lost sight of the proper connection between memorial (anamnesis) and invocation of the Spirit (epiclesis). Each sacrament involves a memorial or re-presentation of the saving events of the past and an invocation of the Holy Spirit. These are not really two separate realities but two sides of the same coin. It is the power of the Spirit that brings about the re-presentation of the saving event, and our "remembering" always entails the invocation of the Spirit. When baptism came to be seen primarily as a "memorial" of Christ's death and resurrection, separated from the invocation of the Spirit, it began to seem necessary to "complete" the baptism by a separate ritual of invoking the Spirit, which we now call confirmation. Hence, what had been two moments of the same celebration of initiation became separated into two independent sacramental rituals.

In a different way, first Eucharist also became detached from baptism. Initially, communion was given to all those baptized.

Even infants were admitted to the Eucharist, and if they were too young to chew the bread, they were given the consecrated wine. This practice was considered normal in the Western Church until the eleventh century. The changing patterns of participation by the laity in the celebration of the Eucharist gradually brought an end to infant communion in the West. As people became focused more on the Eucharistic elements than on the celebration of the Eucharistic meal, concern increased about an infant who might not completely swallow the bread or might spit it up before it was completely digested. With the withdrawal of the cup from the laity in the thirteenth century, infant communion came to an end, and the three sacraments of initiation were no longer clearly linked.

The legalization of Christianity under the emperor Constantine beginning in 313 and the eventual establishment of Christianity as the official religion of the empire sounded the death knell for the catechumenate. Since being a Christian became important for civil status and success, it was not long before almost all adults were Christians and the common experience of baptism was that of children. This process was hastened by the development of the doctrine of original sin, especially under Augustine in the fifth century. It is interesting to note that Augustine seems to use the practice of infant baptism to "prove" the existence of original sin. Since we baptize infants, he insists, and baptism is for the forgiveness of sins, then infants must have some sin to be forgiven. Subsequent generations reversed the argument and began to argue for the necessity of infant baptism because of original sin.

Realizing that the Church was baptizing infants before Augustine developed the doctrine of original sin should remind us that baptism is primarily initiation into the community and into Christ's death and resurrection, not primarily a washing away of sin. The impossibility of a real catechumenate for infants soon reduced it to a few ritual gestures (signing with the cross, the giving of salt, etc.) at the beginning of the baptismal rite.

Missionary work among the Germanic and Slavic tribes in succeeding centuries also contributed to the abandonment of the catechumenate. Mass baptisms of a whole tribe were often conducted upon the decision of the chief to become Christian. Since these tribes were nomadic and largely uneducated, it was difficult to have much of a catechumenate for them—they did not stay in one place long enough!

There were various attempts to reform the Church's initiation pattern in later centuries. The Protestant Reformers put strong emphasis on catechesis for the sacraments. Unfortunately, however, historical knowledge was so limited at the time of the Reformation that they adopted confirmation as a kind of maturity rite. While it was generally not considered a sacrament, it was required for admittance to the Eucharist and became the conclusion of a catechetical process for teens or preteens. This catechetical process is called "the catechumenate" by several Reformation Churches, but the term then refers to postbaptismal, not prebaptismal, catechesis.

Attempts to revive the catechumenate in the Catholic Church were made during the great missionary period of the sixteenth and seventeenth centuries, but these efforts were only minimally successful. It was only in this century, especially in Africa and France, that efforts to revive the catechumenate succeeded. These experiments provided the basis for the universal restoration of the catechumenate in the RCIA, the official Latin text of which was issued in 1972.

QUESTIONS FOR REFLECTION

1. Can you imagine what it must have been like to be a convert to Christianity in the early Church?

2. What similarities and differences can you see between the situation of the Church in the third to the fifth century and our own time?

3. Do you understand why the Church's initiation pattern disintegrated over the centuries? Do you see why a reform was mandated by Vatican Council II?

4. Does a review of this history shed any new light for you on the meaning of baptism? confirmation? first Eucharist?

5. What surprised you most about the history of initiation in the Church?

6. What do you think is the most important point to remember from our past?

CHAPTER TWO

SOME RECENT SHIFTS
IN UNDERSTANDING

The age of reform and renewal in which we live has gene-
rated many new insights and produced some major shifts in
the way the Catholic Church understands itself. This changing self-understanding has immediate ramifications for our
practice of initiation into the community. How a group initiates new members is a clear reflection of how the group
understands its purpose and identity. Thus the renewal of our
initiation policy is a vital part of the renewal of the whole
Church.

Our changing self-understanding can be seen in a variety
of shifts that have become evident since the Second Vatican
Council. One shift concerns the way we understand what happens to an infant who dies before being baptized. For many
centuries great stress was put on baptizing the child as soon
as possible after birth. This approach reflected the high rate
of infant mortality in past centuries, coupled with a fear that
an infant who died could not enter heaven without being
baptized.

The new rite of baptism of children puts much more stress
on the role of the parents and the importance of their faith
in the celebration of baptism. For this reason it suggests
that baptism be postponed if the parents "are not yet prepared
to profess the faith or to undertake the duty of bringing

up their children as Christians." While it is really an ancient understanding that baptism is appropriate only when there is reasonable assurance that the child will be raised in the faith, the necessity of questioning that assumption has increased significantly in recent years as many Catholics have abandoned the practice of the faith but still request the baptism of their children for family or cultural reasons.

The shift from the stress on immediate baptism to an emphasis on parental readiness also presumes a shift in our understanding of what happens to an infant who dies without baptism. Our approach in the past relied heavily on the theological concept of "limbo," a place or state for those who could not enter heaven but did not deserve hell. This concept was never defined doctrine, nor were there any declarations of the magisterium about it, but it was a fairly common theological explanation. The explanation limped a bit, though, because it was also taught that at the end of the world there would only be heaven and hell. Somehow God would have to decide at that point how to deal with the unbaptized who had not sinned. We might say that the concept of limbo today is itself "in limbo." Theologians today seem to approach the question from the assumption of God's mercy at the time of death.

Our official rites also seem to reflect this shift. For the first time in the Church's history, the Sacramentary contains Mass formularies for the funeral of a child who died before baptism. The prayers and the readings of that Mass stress the mercy of God, and the preface is to be taken from the usual prefaces for Christian burial, all of which leads to the implication that the deceased child is somehow "in Christ" and saved by Christ. This rite for the burial of such a child goes so far in that direction that the rubrics include a cautionary note that the "doctrine of the necessity of baptism should not be weakened in the catechesis of the faithful." The rite, therefore, still recognizes the importance of baptism, yet it relies heavily on the mercy of God when a deceased child has not been baptized.

Another shift that has gradually become more apparent since the Council is a shift toward the integral celebration of the sacraments of initiation. The Council fathers had called for making clear the close connection between these sacraments, a mandate that was reflected first in the Rite of Baptism for Children (issued in 1969). The introduction to the Lord's Prayer in that rite clearly points to the other two sacraments of initiation: ". . . these children have been reborn in baptism. They are now called children of God, for so indeed they are. In confirmation they will receive the fullness of God's Spirit. In holy communion they will share the banquet of Christ's sacrifice, calling God their Father in the midst of the Church" (no. 68).

A further step in this shift is evident in the provisions for the minister of confirmation. Prior to the Council, priests could confirm only in the case of an emergency, that is, when a person was in danger of death. In the Rite of Confirmation (issued in 1971), priests are also empowered to confirm in union with the bishop when there are a large number of candidates and to confirm when they "baptize an adult or a child old enough for catechesis or receive a validly baptized adult into full communion with the Church" (no. 7b). This provision is made so that the sacraments of initiation can be celebrated together.

This shift is given further emphasis in the Rite of Christian Initiation of Adults (issued in 1972): "In accord with the ancient practice followed in the Roman liturgy, adults are not to be baptized without receiving confirmation immediately afterward, unless some serious reason stands in the way. The conjunction of the two celebrations signifies the unity of the paschal mystery, the close link between the mission of the Son and the outpouring of the Holy Spirit, and the connection between the two sacraments through which the Son and the

Holy Spirit come with the Father to those who are baptized"
(no. 215). Since these sacraments are celebrated in the context
of the Easter Eucharist, the RCIA pushes us strongly toward
the unified celebration of the three sacraments of initiation.

Whether or when the next step in this process will occur
is uncertain. Perhaps we are moving toward a consistent practice of celebrating these sacraments together, even with infants,
as the Church did for centuries. Perhaps we will continue to
celebrate the sacraments separately when children are being
initiated. But it is clearer today than it has been for centuries
that these sacraments are part of one initiation process and cannot be properly understood except in relation to one another.

The very restoration of the catechumenate in the Church
is itself a shift with vast implications. While we continue—
and will continue for the foreseeable future—to baptize infants,
and although numerically we baptize far more infants than
adults, it is clear that adult initiation is becoming the basic
model by which we understand baptism. The RCIA has been
called the "norm" for baptism, not in the sense that it will be
the normal or most frequent celebration of baptism, but in the
sense that it clarifies for us what baptism means and what is
required for full initiation into the Christian community. Infant baptism is then seen as an adaptation of adult initiation—a
valid adaptation but clearly derivative from the adult model.

Some scholars dispute this point theoretically, but on a practical level it seems clear that the full implementation of both
the Rite of Baptism for Children and the Rite of Christian Initiation of Adults establishes the adult rite as the model from
which people come to understand the meaning of baptism,
conversion, and full initiation. There are several reasons why
this is so. The first is the richness and fullness of the rites of
the RCIA. Because these rites are celebrated in the midst of
the parish community and are linked closely to the conversion
experience of the catechumens, the rituals speak very power-

fully to the whole assembly of the faithful. It is also easy for adults in the assembly to identify with the adults being initiated and thus come to understand their own initiation from an adult perspective. The relative compactness of the initiation process for adults also makes it a more practical model. Although the full process may last two or three years, it is still much more compact than the celebration of the three initiation sacraments spread out over twelve or even eighteen years. The adult initiation process can be more easily recognized as a unified experience and thus becomes a model for understanding initiation.

Finally, the close link between the RCIA experience and the community's observance of Lent and Easter is a significant factor. As the whole community seeks a deeper conversion during Lent and celebrates the renewal of baptismal promises at Easter, the celebration of the rite of election, the scrutinies, and the Easter sacraments with the adult candidates becomes deeply intertwined with the assembly's experience. For these reasons the adult rite naturally becomes the premier experience of baptism in a parish and the model by which initiation is understood, whether it is celebrated in a given case with adults or with children.

These shifts in our understanding of initiation point toward some deeper shifts in our understanding of what it means to be the Church and what membership in the Church entails. Avery Dulles and others have made us aware that there are many different models for understanding the Church itself. Our recent past has been heavily dependent on the institutional model of the Church, with duties, rights, and authority clearly delineated. The current renewal has begun to balance that model with others, such as the Church as servant of the world, as herald of the gospel, as sacrament of Christ's presence in the world, and as a community of disciples. Each of the models adds to our understanding of the Church.

This broader sense of the Church's role also leads to a shift in our understanding of membership in the Church. In the older view, the emphasis was on getting everyone on board and making sure they stayed there until the ship got into port. As long as one didn't fall overboard into mortal sin, he or she would be saved. That model sees the Church much like Noah's ark, saving its passengers from the flood. Today we are learning to see the Church more like a medical mission ship. Such a ship travels the world offering medical services to people in less developed countries. It also has people on board, for it requires a crew. But no one is accepted as part of the crew unless he or she is willing to help carry on the mission of the ship.

Perhaps, theologians suggest today, God does not intend that every human being become a part of the visible Church. God wills the salvation of all people, but perhaps most people will be saved without explicit faith in Christ. Those who are called to such explicit faith form the Church, and they are called to be servants to the world, to carry on the mission of Christ. It is instructive to note that many of the images of the Church in the New Testament suggest the Church as an influential part of the picture but not the whole. The Church is salt but not the whole meal, leaven but not the whole dough, light for the world but not the whole world. Those who are called to membership in the Church are called precisely to a life of service to the world in imitation of their Lord.

It is important to realize the crucial role of the initiation process in the definition of a group's identity and purpose. In any group, the way new members are initiated reflects and shapes the group's self-awareness. Changes in the Church's initiation patterns have a powerful effect in the whole life of the Church. How new Christians are initiated affects not only the identity of those initiated but also the self-understanding of the whole church community. That is why the RCIA is so vitally important to the renewal of the life of the Church in our day.

A few examples of the influence of initiation on the Church's self-understanding may help to clarify the point. Since the RCIA makes it clear that a catechumen is a member of the Church even before baptism, our understanding of both baptism and membership shifts somewhat. The RCIA also presumes that such members have responsibilities for mission and service, which helps to redefine for all members of the Church what being a Christian requires of us. That sense of mission, which is so strong in the RCIA, pushes us to deepen our sense of the Church's purpose in carrying on the work of Christ for the salvation of the world.

The reestablishment of the catechumenate as an "order" within the Church, alongside the order of the faithful, the order of presbyters, the order of deacons, etc., causes a shift in understanding all those other orders, perhaps especially the order of the faithful. And the regular celebration of initiation in the midst of the community provides an opportunity for a constant renewal of baptismal commitment by the whole community.

That may be the most important change in our initiatory practice, for celebrating initiation with the whole assembly gives us once again a regular recourse to the meaning of our membership and the identity of the Church in a way that should lead us to a continuing renewal of our whole Christian life together as Church.

QUESTIONS FOR REFLECTION

1. Has your own understanding of the Church changed since Vatican Council II? In what ways?

2. In what direction do you think the Church should move in regard to the initiation of infants?

3. Has the RCIA become the model from which you personally understand initiation in the Church? Is this true for your parish as a whole?

4. What does it mean to you to be a member of the Church? What criteria should we use to determine when someone is ready to be initiated as a new member?

5. How often does your parish community celebrate the initiation of new members? How well do you celebrate initiation?

6. How does the order of catechumens affect your understanding of other orders in the Church? How does it affect your view of your own order?

CHAPTER THREE

PATTERNS OF INITIATION

The sacraments of the Church enable us to share in divine realities, but they are fashioned from human symbols and operate on basic human principles. It is reasonable to assume, then, that our understanding of the sacraments of initiation will benefit from an investigation into initiation patterns in other groups and societies.

In 1909, Arnold van Gennep published his landmark study entitled *Rites de Passage*. In this work he delineated three stages in any rite of passage. The first is a movement of separation from the previous social group or social state of those going through the passage. This is followed by a period of transition, a liminal or threshold state in which the candidates are betwixt and between—they no longer belong to the previous group but have not yet been accepted into the new state either. The passage concludes with a movement of aggregation or entrance into the new group or social state.

Rites of passage can be of many types, including coming-of-age or puberty rites, installation rituals, marriage rituals, etc. They can involve a transition up or down the social ladder or a lateral move to a different social role. They can be brief or extensive, simple or complex, primitive or sophisticated, but they always involve the same three movements.

Mircea Eliade, an anthropologist long associated with the University of Chicago, did extensive studies on initiation rites during his lifetime. He defines initiation as "a body of rites and oral teachings whose purpose is to produce a decisive alteration in the religious and social status of the person to be initiated" (*Rites and Symbols of Initiation* [Harper, 1958], p. x). It is the community's conception of the world that is revealed in its initiation rites, Eliade insists. It is in its initiation rituals that a community hands on its values and its way of life. In the process of expressing and communicating those basic values and meanings, the whole community is renewed in its own identity and commitments.

Eliade also notes the importance of an ordeal in the initiation process. It is primarily the ordeal, he insists, that constitutes the religious experience of initiation, the encounter with the sacred. This is an important point to remember when we get nervous about the demands that the RCIA makes on candidates for initiation.

The Liminal Period

Victor Turner has continued Eliade's work and has focused extensively on the central stage of Van Gennep's three stages, the liminal period. In his book *The Forest of Symbols* (Cornell Univ. Press, 1967), Turner delineates several characteristics of the liminal period. The first is an invisibility, either real or structural. Sometimes the initiates are removed from the group and hidden away in a special building or a secluded place. At other times they may simply be ignored socially, even though they are physically present in the village. It is common that the initiates are all called by the same name. They have no rights of property ownership. They may be symbolized as dead or unborn, and sometimes sex distinctions are obliterated by a common garb or even some physical mutilation. The net result of all this is a submerging of individuality and individual social status into the group.

Turner also notes the frequency of ambiguous symbolism connected with the liminal period. Some of the more common symbols used are the tomb-womb, symbolizing both death and rebirth; the moon, which waxes and wanes; the snake, which seems to die as it sheds its skin but continues to live with a new skin; the bear, which hibernates through the winter and seems to be reborn in the spring; and nakedness, which is the condition of both the corpse and the newborn. Since the liminal period is a time betwixt and between, the ambiguous symbols are a natural means to express the ambiguous nature of the period.

The liminal period is a very precious time in many tribal cultures. Especially in societies in which daily survival requires constant effort, the opportunity for reflection and pondering life's mysteries is rare. The liminal period, with its absence of social roles, is also a time without social obligations. The initiates are free to think and to contemplate the meaning of life and the order of things in creation. This is the function of some of the strange images we see in museums and anthropology books. Images combining human and animal features can provoke reflection on the similarities and differences between humans and animals. Human figures with exaggerated body parts might foster consideration of the purpose and value of those parts. The liminal period of the initiation process offers the opportunity and the freedom to think deeply about life, a fact that should be remembered in considering the catechumenate.

Thinking of the liminal period as a "threshold" period also raises some intriguing connections with the idea of a "threshold experience." Many saints and mystics through the ages, as well as ordinary people in every age, have described experiences when earth and heaven seemed to meet, when time stood still, and when God seemed almost tangibly present to them. These experiences, often called "threshold experiences" because they seem to occur on the threshold between earth and heaven, would be of obvious value in the initiation process. While no one can orchestrate such an occurrence, it seems very possible that being in a liminal period could leave a candidate more open to such an encounter with the divine. This is so because the liminal period allows a kind of freedom from the usual routines and responsibilities, enabling the candidate to focus in different directions than he or she usually does.

Another factor that might make a candidate more open to a threshold experience might be precisely the separation from the comfort of one's usual lifestyle. Entering a liminal period involves a stripping of one's defenses and an abandonment of the roles by which we usually define ourselves. This can be profoundly unsettling, and the resulting sense of dislocation may actually leave the candidate more open to a new way of experiencing life and reality, or to experiencing reality on a new level. This openness is often the key ingredient that is missing in our ordinary lives, and its lack may prevent us from profoundly experiencing God's presence on a more regular basis.

In discussing the internal structure of the liminal period, Turner notes that there is usually a complete submission to the instructors, along with a complete equality among the initiates. All social status has been lost, and all are equally subject to the instructors. The son of the chief of the tribe and the son of the lowest man on the totem pole are equal as initiates.

This sense of equality and the absence of social distinctions help to create an experience that Turner calls "communitas." This concept is developed especially in his book *The Ritual Process* (Aldine, 1969). Turner probably uses the Latinized term to avoid some of the many divergent meanings that have been attached to the word "community" in recent years. By *communitas* Turner means an experience of unity and solidarity that flows from a shared experience of ultimate reality and a common spirit of cooperation. This experience of *communitas* is possible only when the status and role distinctions of the social structure are transcended. It is thus frequently created in the liminal state, with its deliberate elimination of social distinctions.

Communitas and Social Structure

Communitas is thus contrasted with the social structure, and these two are in a constant dialectical tension. In some ways the experience of *communitas* is a threat to the social structure, since it ignores all roles and status on which the structure depends. It is easily seen as dangerous and anarchical, so the structure seeks to contain and control it with laws, rules, and restrictions. On the other hand, a social structure can become so rigid that it becomes deadening rather than life-supporting. Such a stultifying social structure can be renewed by an outbreak of *communitas*. Regular experiences of *communitas* keep the structure from becoming too rigid and deadly.

The history of the 1960s and '70s in the United States offers an example of this dynamic. A social and political structure that had gotten a bit too rigid in the 1950s was confronted by several manifestations of *communitas*. One of the most obvious was the "hippie" movement. It manifested many of the characteristics that Turner has described for the liminal period. There was a radical equality and an abolition of gender distinctions. There was a rejection of social status and an abandonment of structural roles. Sometimes there were name changes and submission to a guru or some other unquestioned authority figure in a commune situation.

The threat to the social structure was instinctively perceived by many in our society, and attempts were rapidly made to restrict the growth and activity of the communes. Since *communitas* cannot exist long in a pure form, within the movement itself roles and structures gradually developed. In time the "hippie" movement largely died out, but not before it had significantly influenced the social structure, broadening outlooks and bringing legitimacy to many previously unacceptable lifestyles and options for society. This is the fundamental dynamic: *communitas* loosens and invigorates the social structure, while the structure gives form and stability to the *communitas* experience.

Another good example of an outbreak of *communitas* can be seen in the life of St. Francis of Assisi. Francis and his "little brothers" show many of the marks of the *communitas* experience or a liminal group. They owned nothing, abandoned all social status and roles, were submissive to Francis (as well as to the Pope and ultimately to the Lord), shared a common dress, and were united in a close brotherhood. This was clearly a threat to the structure. Francis' way was very attractive to many, and local bishops began to complain that so many were following Francis that they were afraid there would not be enough vocations for the structured Church. Soon Rome required some modifications of the Franciscan movement, insisting that the brothers own their own buildings held in common, etc. But this was not a real attack on the Franciscans. Such a pure form of *communitas* could not survive long without some structure to support it, and Rome provided that. The net result is that few if any Franciscans live today just as Francis lived, but the movement has survived for centuries and has influenced the larger Church permanently with Francis' ideal of poverty and simplicity and communion with nature.

It is also intriguing to note that Christianity itself has something of a permanent liminal character. We are in the world but not "of the world." We are pilgrims in a strange land, with no place to lay our heads. We have here no lasting city. We strive to experience *communitas* in communion with the Lord and one another, and from this perspective we continually critique the social structures within which we live, calling for change and adaptation whenever the structure oppresses or violates values we cherish. While the Church clearly has its own social structure, there is a sense in which it is never as comfortable with that structure as other social groups may be.

Within the Church, too, religious orders manifest many of the marks of a liminal group. This may have been more obvious in pre-Vatican II days, when members were given new names upon entering the order, wore a common dress, gave absolute submission to authority, and lived a strong communal lifestyle. Some have suggested that, in the period of history when the Church had no functioning catechumenate, the religious orders served as a substitute catechumenate, seeking to produce a conversion to full membership in the Church by their novitiates and by their lifestyle. In point of fact, religious did come to be seen by most people as the "real Christians," those who took the gospel seriously and were truly "religious."

The renewal of Vatican II, with its emphasis on the universal call of all Christians to holiness, has begun a major shift in our understanding of religious orders precisely because it challenges all members of the Church to be truly religious and deeply converted. The restoration of the catechumenate is a major factor in that shift, for it seeks to produce an order of the faithful that is as spiritual and committed as only priests and nuns and brothers were expected to be in years past.

Contemporary Rites of Passage

Besides studying exotic tribal rites of passage and initiations, we may find it enlightening to examine some contemporary rites of passage in our own society. Catechumenate teams might learn some things, for example, from the Jewish coming-of-age rites of bar mitzvah or the initiation rites of groups like the Knights of Columbus, the Elks, or the Masons. These groups all have standard ways of initiating new members, sometimes with multiple stages, such as the "degrees" of the Knights of Columbus. Such rites are often somewhat secretive, revealed only to the initiates, and they are usually highly symbolic and traditional.

Another example can be seen in the sometimes outlandish initiation rites of college fraternities and sororities. Why do people do the crazy things that are required to join such groups? Because that's the way you get in, that's the way everybody does it. And going through the experience creates a common bond with all the others who have been through it before. In a more disciplined fashion, cadets at West Point and the other military academies are clearly liminal groups. They are no longer civilians but are not yet officers. During their liminal formation period they have few social distinctions, are subject to absolute authority, wear the same uniforms, etc.

In a less structured but no less real example, consider the experience of engagement and marriage. While engaged, a man and woman are clearly in a liminal stage. They are not yet married, but they are not really single either. The engagement ring signifies a promise to one another, accompanied by a certain lack of freedom to date others (separation), but they are not numbered among the married yet (aggregation). They are clearly betwixt and between (liminal).

In a similar vein, the new driver with a temporary license is set apart from those too young to drive, yet is not considered a driver in his or her own right. Another licensed driver must be in the car whenever the new driver practices. With the completion of the driver's test and the granting of a permanent license, the liminal state is left behind and the new driver enters the ranks of the full-fledged driving public. Notice the power of this "rite of passage" in shaping the young person's sense of identity as a "grown-up" in our society. It is often a major transition point in adolescent development.

A final area that deserves examination includes groups like Alcoholics Anonymous, which are, especially in the early stages of membership, liminal experiences as a person leaves one identity behind and gradually takes on a new lifestyle. It could be very helpful for catechumenate teams to consider how such groups foster that kind of change of life and to relate that process to the challenge of fostering Christian conversion in the catechumenate.

In examining all these different manifestations of rites of passage, we should be continually asking ourselves just what is needed for a person to *really* become a part of a community. Conversion of life and true initiation into the community of faith are the two main goals of the liminal period we call the catechumenate.

QUESTIONS FOR REFLECTION

1. Can you name some rites of passage in your own life?
2. Can you recall living through some liminal periods in your transitions? How did it feel? What would have helped you then?
3. What kinds of "ordeals" did you experience in these transitions? Did they intensify the experience or make it more memorable?
4. Can you see now the growth that these passages fostered in your personal history? Was this clear to you in the midst of the experience?
5. How do you personally deal with the tension between *communitas* and structure? Is it a creative tension in your own life?
6. Do you think your catechumenate team could learn anything from other contemporary experiences of initiation?

CHAPTER FOUR

THE MEANING OF CONVERSION

The theme of the new puzzle we are called to assemble is conversion. We are called by the Rite of Christian Initiation of Adults to become a Church whose central dynamic is conversion. The term "conversion" has a rich and crucial history in the life of the Christian community, but it is a term that has often been misunderstood in recent times. Most Catholics tend to think that conversion applies only to people who "convert" from one Christian denomination to another. But conversion is a lifelong challenge for every member of the Church. It is a matter of allowing God to work in us, gradually converting our lives more and more to gospel values, shaping us more and more into the image of Christ.

While conversion is a lifelong task, it is the special dynamic of those who are in a liminal period. Various writers have described the conversion experience as primarily the experience of crisis. Often it is a personal crisis of some kind that provokes the beginnings of conversion. There is usually some sense of setting out, of leaving behind the normal and usual way of doing things or seeing things. The experience itself is one of adventure as one explores new territory both in oneself and in the world at large. The conclusion of the experience is marked by a sense of return, perhaps to a new place or perhaps to the same place, but as it was never known before. These three stages clearly correspond to the rites-of-passage stages of separation, liminal period, and reaggregation. Using the language of the adventure, however, casts new light on the concept that conversion is a journey; it is often the adventure trip of a lifetime.

The role of ritual on such a journey is threefold. Rituals help to mediate the process, giving some direction to the journey. They help to name the experience, clarifying what is happening to the traveler. And rituals thus help to moderate the instinctive fear of change that we all seem to have, for they reassure us that others have traveled this way before us successfully and that the journey does have an end.

The primary image of this journey in the Christian context is the death and resurrection of Jesus. The setting out always means a kind of death to the past and to the usual. The return is a beginning of a new life, a resurrection. And the journey itself is a passover, an adventure of movement from the old to the new, from sin to grace, from death to life.

The Catholic tradition has always seen conversion basically as a gradual process rather than as an affair of a particular moment. There may well be special moments on our conversion journey when God touches us powerfully and deeply. But such moments come after some process of preparation has been occurring, and there has to be some form of follow-up if the conversion is to be lasting. Hence most Catholics cannot name the day on which they were "saved" or the exact moment of their conversion. The fact that conversion generally occurs gradually, however, does not mean that it is any less real or deep than St. Paul's getting knocked off his horse on the way to Damascus. No matter how or when it occurs, conversion is always the work of God's grace, the result of God's power at work within us.

Conversion can be defined as a radical transformation of life as a result of personal contact with the living God. As such, conversion involves many different dimensions. It includes acquiring new knowledge and new ways of understanding the mysteries of life. It entails changes in one's moral life, turning away from sin and developing habits of virtue. It involves spiritual growth and a developing prayer life. It encompasses psychological dimensions that may run very deep. And it has social implications, affecting the way we deal with others and the priority of different relationships in our lives.

Intellectual Conversion

Let us consider each of those dimensions briefly in turn. The intellectual component of the conversion process has been well emphasized in recent Catholic experience. The old inquiry classes and catechisms tended to approach initiation into the Church almost entirely as a matter of learning sufficient doctrine. More recent trends have played down the doctrinal component, sometimes overreacting to the overemphasis of the past. The balance here may be difficult to find and maintain. If the catechumenate offers a true initiation into adult Christian life, it should result in a lifelong desire to learn and grow in faith. Thus it should not be necessary to "cover" everything in the catechumenate.

On the other hand, it is important to remember that the catechumenate in its classical period was the place where serious theology was developed. The catechumenate is not a watered-down Sunday school class but a place where the hard questions of life will be probed and discussed. As in tribal initiations, the catechumenate should offer the freedom to reflect deeply on the meaning of life and the ultimate mysteries. It should be a time when hard questions are asked and probed. There may not be easy answers for many of these questions, but that is the kind of serious intellectual struggle that a good catechumenate requires.

Conversion of Behavior

The moral challenges of conversion are perhaps the ones most people assume will be central when a person converts from a position of no faith in God. The image of a gangster converting to God on his deathbed conjures up a sense of high drama. But when the person converting is already a Christian, many people tend to assume that there does not have to be much change in moral lifestyle. Yet the call to conversion is a call to a radical transformation of life, to a radical freedom from sin, and to a total lifestyle of loving service.

None of us ever really completes that transformation in this life, so the call to moral conversion is always relevant. Sometimes we minimize this dimension because we look only at the more obvious and dramatic personal sins. As long as a person is not committing murder or adultery, we conclude that he or she is morally upright. Yet all of us are involved in sinful situations, some personal and some social. Some may be obvious, but many are subtle and have worked their way into the very fabric of our lives and our society. We are continually being seduced by the values of our society and the many "isms" that mark our culture: consumerism, narrow nationalism, egotism, militarism, sexism, racism, etc. The call to conversion is a call to freedom from all those false values, a call to a transformation of life that is truly "radical," in the original sense of that word. "Radical" comes from the Latin *radix*, meaning "root," and it is a long and difficult task to root out from our lives the subtle influences that prevent us from fully living the gospel.

Spiritual Conversion

It should be obvious by now that the spiritual dimension of conversion is closely linked to the moral aspects of the process. It is the work of God's Spirit within us that sets us free from all those false values and influences. Growth in responsiveness to the Holy Spirit is the core of the spiritual dimension of conversion. The development of a consistent prayer life is a basic necessity for living the gospel day by day. The catechumenate should offer a variety of prayer experiences so that the candidates can find a style or styles of prayer which are comfortable and which promote continued growth in the Spirit. The guidance of a personal spiritual director can be extremely helpful in developing a personal spirituality that is integrated with all the dimensions of a person's life.

These spiritual issues call for a deep spirituality on the part of the catechumenate team. The work of conversion is not our work but the work of God's Spirit. The task of the catechumenate team is to facilitate or foster the work of the Spirit, a task that requires an openness to the Spirit and a sensitivity to God's promptings. If the team members are truly in touch with the Lord in their own lives, they will be able to sense the presence and guidance of the Spirit in the lives of the catechumens as well.

We all have much to learn yet in this area of fostering conversion and facilitating the action of the Spirit. We need to ask ourselves how we can really share our faith, not just doctrines. We need to learn how to lead people toward the threshold where God can be met, how we open people to the possibility of a personal experience of Christ. We need to ask ourselves how we can really teach others to pray and how we can help them learn to interpret life from a gospel perspective.

Little of this can be accomplished just by imparting information. It requires a full process of formation that leads the candidates to Christ while leaving them free to decide how and to what extent they will respond. That is what a true catechumenate is intended to provide.

Psychological Dimensions

The psychological dimensions of conversion need considerable attention in the catechumenate process. If conversion truly entails a radical transformation of life, then it will have deep ramifications psychologically. There are a variety of ways of understanding the psychological implications of conversion.

Any time there is a significant change in a person's life, a process of grief is triggered. Leaving behind a way of life, a church, or a group of friends entails a real loss, so a catechumen may well need to grieve to some degree. If so, the catechumen will likely experience some or all of the stages of grief that have been described by writers like Elizabeth Kübler-Ross. Since one's religion is a major factor in a person's self-identity, one's image of oneself, the shift required in conversion also means a major change in the way a catechumen identifies himself or herself.

Significant changes in a person's life always create some measure of anxiety. Psychologists have long noted that one's anxiety level tends to rise in a cumulative fashion if several major changes occur in a given space of time. A catechumen who is also preparing for marriage or changing jobs or dealing with the loss of a loved one could well find the challenge of conversion producing a high level of anxiety.

Major shifts may occur in familiar patterns of life or prayer or worship, as well as in relationships with family members or friends. Some catechumens experience serious opposition from, or rejection by, relatives who do not understand their desire to join the Catholic Church or who may have strong antagonism toward Catholics. This opposition can cause deep pain and difficult decisions for those who feel called by God to join the Church. It's a painful example of the sword of division that Christ said he came to bring (see Matthew 10:34-35).

Finally, catechumens who deeply examine their lives and attitudes may find that they have some work to do in healing relationships or healing memories from earlier in life. I remember one woman who came to me in the first or second year that I worked with the RCIA. We had regular interviews with the catechumens to keep in touch with their progress and growth. When I asked her what else was happening in her life while she was involved with all the meetings and prayer and relationships of the catechumenate, she said, "Well, I've started to go to a psychiatrist."

Hesitantly I asked, "Oh . . . uh . . . ah . . . because of the catechumenate?"

"Yes," she replied, "we've been talking about forgiveness in our sessions and I've discovered that I've never really forgiven my parents for the way they raised me. I knew I couldn't deal with that alone, so I decided to get help."

I realized then that this woman was really going through a conversion at a deep level, that God was working with her and leading her to the healing of her past hurts. I have often said, only half-jokingly, that a large parish with a fully functioning catechumenate may need to hire a full-time psychologist for the staff!

In any case, it is crucial that both sponsors and the catechumenate team be sensitive to these psychological dimensions of conversion if they are to properly guide the catechumens on their conversion journey.

The Importance of the Ordeal

When we examined Mircea Eliade's work on initiation, we noted his contention that the ordeal is the primary factor in creating the religious experience in initiation. It may be helpful to consider briefly the psychological dynamics involved in an ordeal and see how they might apply to the catechumenate.

First of all, an ordeal emphasizes the importance of the process. It says that what the candidate is doing is worth the effort. In theological terms, it reminds us that there is no "cheap grace." Grace is a gift, of course, but it also calls us to conversion, which makes significant demands on us.

Secondly, the ordeal provides a sense of movement and, ultimately, of completion. When a candidate has completed the ordeal, he or she has a sense of progress in the initiation experience.

Thirdly, going through the ordeal gives a sense of identity with the group that is not obtained any other way. There is a special bond between people who have been through an ordeal together, as well as with all those who experienced the ordeal at an earlier time. Like the fraternity or sorority initiations, ordeals are a matter of some pride and accomplishment, and they convey a deep sense of belonging when they are completed.

The ordeals of the catechumenate may vary for different catechumens. For some it may be the challenge of standing before the congregation for the various rituals. For others it may entail a verbal witness to the way God is working in their lives. For others it may simply be the length of the initiation process and the denial of the privilege of receiving communion until the process is completed.

Whatever the ordeal is, it is very important not to short-circuit its power by minimizing it. There is a temptation to try to make initiation as easy as possible for those joining the Church. If a catechumen finds some part of the process difficult, a sponsor or team member may feel that it should be omitted or simplified or shortened somehow. While it is necessary at times to make adaptations in the initiation process to meet the true spiritual needs of individual candidates, we should be very hesitant to change the process just because it seems difficult or makes demands on the catechumens. Conversion is not easy, and the difficulty of the process can be very important psychologically in deepening the religious experience of initiation.

There is need for a careful balance between a sensitivity to true limitations and needs of the catechumens and a firmness about the demands of the initiation process. We have to remember always that initiation's power to convey a true sense of belonging flows to a significant degree from the sense that this is the way one joins. Too many exceptions can vitiate the sense of truly becoming a part of something important and something much greater than personal needs or wishes.

Process and Ritual

The importance of conversion in the initiation process cannot be overemphasized. Conversion is the basic dynamic of initiation into the Church, and the process of conversion provides the basis for all the rituals of the catechumenate. It is important not to think of rituals as independent moments that somehow work miracles on people. The rituals of the catechumenate are intended to be expressions of the underlying process that God is bringing about in the lives of the catechumens. The rituals have little meaning or value unless they express a conversion process that is truly occurring.

That is not to say that rituals have no effects. The celebration of the rites will both reinforce and further the underlying conversion by focusing the process and offering the community's support. But those effects depend on the ritual having a real base in the lives of those around whom the community celebrates. Otherwise, what the rituals proclaim is not true, and the rites become empty symbols that ring hollow and have little effect.

The focus on the conversion of the catechumens is obviously central, yet it is also crucial to remember that the liturgy is always the celebration of the whole community. The community often celebrates around an individual or a group, but the whole assembly must bring their own lived experience to the celebration. Thus the RCIA calls not only the catechumens but also the whole community to embrace the dynamic of conversion in their own lives.

It is for this reason that many commentators have noted that the RCIA offers the strongest "tool" we have for the revitalization of the Church as a whole. By making the conversion journey of the catechumens a public process, the RCIA invites the whole community to share with them in this journey of continual conversion. The witness of the catechumens themselves and their willingness to share their experience with others is more powerful than a whole series of sermons calling the congregation to conversion. The initiation of new members is truly "the responsibility of all the baptized" (RCIA, no. 9), for all share the same call to conversion of life and carrying on the work of Christ in the world today.

QUESTIONS FOR REFLECTION

1. Do you think of yourself as a convert? Are you letting God transform your life more and more?

2. Can you recognize in the catechumens in your parish the same dynamics of conversion you experience in your own faith journey?

3. How can we foster the conversion process in candidates for initiation? What helps you to grow in Christ?

4. What dimensions of conversion does your parish foster best? Which dimensions need more attention?

5. What "ordeals" have you seen catechumens experience? How can you help them without vitiating the power of the initiation process?

6. Do you understand the role of rituals in the initiation process? What does each of the rituals of the RCIA express?

CHAPTER FIVE

UNDERSTANDING THE RCIA

In the last chapter we described the rituals of the Rite of Christian Initiation of Adults as expressions of the underlying process of conversion in the lives of the catechumens. This perspective puts the primary emphasis on the process rather than on the rituals, which is an important insight for those of us who have perhaps understood the sacraments in the past as rituals that somehow produced effects almost magically through God's grace. Thomas Aquinas in the thirteenth century insisted that sacraments "cause by signifying."

Remembering that fact should lead us to be concerned about the authenticity of the symbols that we make in our rituals. The power of the sacrament to touch us and change us depends to a great degree on whether the symbols we make truly reflect the reality they speak.

Another way of saying this is to note that God works in our lives in a myriad of ways and that sacraments are intended to focus our attention upon and to celebrate that ongoing work of God in us. The sacraments are like mountain peaks along the journeys of our lives. From their height we can look back and see where God has been active in our lives and look ahead to where God still calls us to go.

The sacraments enable us—to change images for a moment—to hold up the mystery of God's action in our lives to the light and examine and marvel at the beauty of the gem that is God's grace at work in us. Wondering at the mystery and gaining the perspective of the mountaintop both contribute to the furtherance of the process, for we are drawn even closer to God and see more clearly where the Spirit is leading us. Thus sacraments do have effects on us, especially to the extent that they are integral parts of the ongoing journey of our spiritual lives.

This emphasis on the process is extremely important for a proper understanding of the Rite of Christian Initiation of Adults. There is a strong temptation to look at the RCIA as simply a collection of new rituals and rubrics to be implemented in our worship services. To approach it this way is to try to put the new puzzle piece into an old puzzle. The RCIA calls for a much broader view of initiation and of all the sacraments than most of us have had in the past. The integration of process and rituals is central to the design of the RCIA, and the proper implementation of the rite must begin with that realization.

At the same time, once we understand the importance of the process, it is not invalid to view the RCIA as a series of rituals and the preparation that leads to them. This perspective has two very important ramifications. The first is that the rituals are important, too, and need to be carried out and celebrated with all the richness and care that we can muster. The second is that we can gain some understanding of the process required for each section of the RCIA by examining the ritual to which it leads and asking ourselves what is needed to make the words and actions of the celebration a true expression of what has happened in the lives of the catechumens up to that point. If the ritual speaks a message that those who are celebrating it cannot speak honestly from their own experience, then the process has not yet arrived at the point where it makes sense to celebrate the ritual. So the process must be designed and implemented in a way that will enable both the catechumens and the whole community to celebrate the rites honestly and fruitfully.

With that in mind, let us examine the various periods and steps of the Rite of Christian Initiation of Adults, first in a general overview and then examining each period and step individually. The full rite consists of four periods, with the transitions between each period marked by a ritual step.

The first period is called the precatechumenate. It is a time for evangelization, for inquiry and introduction to the gospel, a time for the beginnings of faith. When the candidates are ready to make the decision to join the Church, the community celebrates the rite of acceptance into the order of catechumens. This rite makes them members of the Church, not as baptized members of the order of the faithful but as members of the order of catechumens.

The second period, then, is the period of the catechumenate proper. This period may last several years and is a time of catechesis and formation. It includes instruction, a growing familiarity with the Christian way of life, prayer and various liturgical celebrations, and service to others. The second step, which concludes this period, is the rite of election or enrollment of names for the Easter sacraments. Usually celebrated by the bishop on the First Sunday of Lent, this rite indicates the Church's judgment that the catechumens are ready to enter the order of the faithful at the Easter Vigil.

The election leads into the third period, called purification and enlightenment. This is an intense time of spiritual growth, a kind of retreat in preparation for the celebration of the sacraments. It is marked by the celebration of the scrutinies on the Third, Fourth, and Fifth Sundays of Lent and by the presentations of the Creed and the Lord's Prayer. The third step is the celebration of the sacraments of baptism, confirmation, and Eucharist at the Easter Vigil. By these initiation sacraments the candidates enter the order of the faithful and take on responsibility for the full mission of the Church.

The fourth and final period extends throughout the Easter season, from Easter Sunday to Pentecost. It is the period of postbaptismal catechesis, or mystagogy, and is a time for deepening the Christian experience and entering more fully into the life of the faithful.

The rite urges continuing meetings for the neophytes (newly baptized) throughout the year following Pentecost, concluding with a celebration of the first anniversary of their baptism.

The Precatechumenate

The first period of the RCIA, the period of the pre-catechumenate or evangelization, is perhaps the most difficult one to handle. It is in some ways a rather vague period, which makes its planning somewhat problematic. It is described in the rite as consisting of "inquiry on the part of the candidates and of evangelization and the precatechumenate on the part of the Church" (no. 7). In the outline of the RCIA it is called "a time of no fixed duration or structure, for inquiry and introduction to Gospel values, an opportunity for the beginnings of faith." Technically the period is not even part of the rite of initiation, which begins with admission to the catechumenate. It is *pre*-catechumenate, pre-initiation, but it is called a time of great importance.

Part of our difficulty in dealing with this period comes from its indeterminate length and structure. Some people have been in a kind of precatechumenate for years, taking inquiry classes or going to Mass with a spouse or talking with members of the Church. Only after a long search do they come to a decision to become Catholic, to join the Church and be baptized. How do we structure such a search? Moreover, those who do come seeking to learn more about the Church come with very diverse backgrounds. Some are ready to launch right into the catechumenate, while others have just started to search for God. Once the catechumenate proper begins, the group has at least the common denominator of having made the decision to join the Church.

Another reason why we may find this period difficult is that it calls for evangelization, and Catholics generally have not been very strong in that field. It is a time for proclaiming the gospel, for presenting the living God and Jesus Christ who has been sent for our salvation. For a long time, at least in this country, the Catholic Church has been much better at ministry to those who already believe than it has at preaching the gospel to the unconverted. We have built a great parochial school system and strong religious education programs, provided hospitals and nursing homes, sponsored and guided immigrants and refugees, and developed a wide variety of social service agencies, but when it comes to simply preaching the gospel, we often seem to be tongue-tied.

Father Vincent Donovan, in his book *Christianity Rediscovered* (Fides/Claretian, 1978), tells of a radical decision he made as a missionary to the Masai in Africa. After many years of operating mission schools and hospitals, missionaries could count very few converts among the Masai. So Father Donovan decided to leave the mission compounds behind and preach the gospel to the Masai as simply and as directly as he could. The response of the Masai elders to him was very interesting.

"If that is why you came here," they asked, "why did you wait so long to tell us about this?" People are often anxious to hear the Good News preached to them. The RCIA calls us to become once again an evangelizing Church.

We may also find the precatechumenate difficult because we are easily tempted to short-circuit the process by moving too quickly to acceptance into the order of catechumens. This is due partly to an attempt to schedule the full process of initiation within the school year. This leads to the necessity of moving into the order of catechumens before Christmas, leaving only a few weeks for the precatechumenate period. But this hurry can also be the result of an inadequate understanding of what is supposed to happen during the precatechumenate. The rite speaks of this period as providing an opportunity for the inquirers to come to believe, to be converted, and to commit themselves to the Lord. The evangelization of this period should lead to faith and initial conversion, with a gradual maturing of the will to follow Christ and seek baptism.

It is important to realize that the step which marks the end of this period is a major step in the life of the candidates. By becoming catechumens, they enter the Church. Thus the precatechumenate is not complete until they are able to decide whether they want to be members of the Church or not. It often takes great patience to wait upon the Spirit until such a decision is clear and firm. To move into the catechumenate proper before such a decision can honestly be made is to miss the great importance of this first period.

A basic problem with the precatechumenate confronts us in the pluralistic society of the United States. The Rite of Christian Initiation of Adults follows the ancient pattern, which developed in a time when there was a basic unity in the Church. We, however, live in an age with over a thousand different denominations of Christianity.

So the decision to enter "the Church" also involves a decision as to which denomination of the Church one wishes to enter. For this reason it seems that more than pure evangelization may be required for inquirers to make the decision necessary to enter the catechumenate proper. Beyond hearing the gospel, people may need to understand how different Churches live out that gospel and why there are these differences.

On the other hand, we should be careful not to raise difficulties in this area unnecessarily. It is often the case that persons are drawn to a particular church community precisely because they are attracted to the way it lives the gospel. Living in this pluralistic society, they may have already sensed that this community is the one to which God is calling them. Then the issue becomes more clearly the question of true conversion of heart and life to Christ. While conversion is a life-long task, and even this first conversion must continue to develop throughout the catechumenate, it is still important to discern a true conversion and initial faith in the inquirers before admitting them into the order of catechumens.

Admission to the Catechumenate

The first ritual step of the RCIA is the rite of acceptance into the order of catechumens. This rite is to take place on specified days throughout the year, and the RCIA says two, or if necessary three, such days are to be fixed as the usual time for this celebration (no. 18.3).

The celebration should take place with the entire Christian community or at least some part of it. In this rite the Church "carries out its apostolic mission" (no. 41), bringing men and women to Christ and adding them to the household of the faith.

The rite begins with the reception of the candidates, including their acceptance of the gospel and signing them with the cross on the forehead and the senses. At the discretion of the local bishop, this may also include the presentation of a cross or some other symbolic act of reception into the community. After their reception the candidates share in the celebration of the liturgy of the Word of God, which includes intercessions for them and possibly the presentation of Bibles to them. If the Eucharist is to be celebrated on this occasion, the new catechumens are dismissed to their own assembly "to share their joy and spiritual experiences" (no. 67). At the option of the local bishop, the rite of acceptance into the order of catechumens may also include an exorcism and renunciation of false worship and/or the giving of a new name, but it is not expected that these rites will be used often in the United States.

It is important to understand fully the significance of this step. It is, in a real sense, an entrance into the Church. After the celebration of this rite the names of the catechumens are inscribed in the Book of the Catechumens, along with the names of their sponsors and the minister and the date and place of the celebration. As members of the order of catechumens, they are members of the Church, part of the household of Christ (no. 47). They have rights to Christian marriage and Christian burial, and they bear some measure of responsibility for ministry in the Church as well. Recognizing the importance of this step can help us to understand more fully what must be accomplished during the period of the precatechumenate.

The Period of the Catechumenate

The period of the catechumenate is the central period of the RCIA. The rite indicates that this period can vary in length, but it "should be long enough—several years if necessary—for the conversion and faith of the catechumens to become strong" (no. 76). The national statutes approved by the bishops of the United States call for this period to begin before Lent of one year and last until Lent of the following year, or at least from Easter of one year to Lent of the next year (no. 6). This implies at least a two-year approach, since the precatechumenate, the period of enlightenment, and the postbaptismal catechesis are in addition to this full-year catechumenate period.

Many parishes have begun use of the RCIA on a school-year model, including the precatechumenate and all three subsequent periods in the time from September to Pentecost. Practical experience has indicated that this is too short a time to allow for the depth and breadth of growth that the Rite of Christian Initiation of Adults requires. Many parishes will need to rethink and expand their programs in light of the new national statutes. Parishes that are just beginning to use the RCIA might start with a one-year schema, but they should be planning to move toward fuller implementation as soon as that is feasible.

What is to occur during this lengthy period? There are four principal dimensions to the catechumenate proper. The first is instruction or catechesis. Though this is the dimension most of us find familiar, it is in some ways the most difficult to do well. The RCIA calls for a catechesis that is "gradual and complete in its coverage, accommodated to the liturgical year, and solidly supported by celebrations of the word" (no. 75.1). This is not a new approach for the Church, but it is new when compared with our recent history, especially in its insistence that the catechesis should be accommodated to the liturgical year. At the very least, this suggests that we don't study the birth of Christ in the middle of Lent or deal with penance during the Easter season. More positively, it calls for a closer relationship between our catechetical efforts and our worship life. For centuries most of our catechesis, whether of children or of adults, was conducted in the context of the community's annual cycle of worship celebrations. A return to this approach tends to link our catechetical efforts more closely to the Word of God as it is proclaimed to us in the liturgy. This is a desirable goal in all our catechesis, not just in the Rite of Christian Initiation of Adults, but it is starting there. Various publications have begun to appear that outline an approach to catechesis based on the Sunday Lectionary, which seems to be the most obvious way to stay in touch with the liturgical cycle. This also provides a natural link between the catechetical sessions and the Sunday reflection on the Word of God following the dismissal from the Eucharistic assembly.

The insistence that the catechesis should be "gradual and complete in its coverage" needs to be properly understood. There is a tendency at times to think that a catechumen must know everything that a lifelong Catholic knows. That is both unrealistic and misguided. The catechumen is on a journey of initiation and conversion. Even after the catechumenate is completed, the newly baptized are called "neophytes," or newborns. We need to nurture in the catechumens a recognition that being a Christian requires lifelong learning. They should not expect or be expected to be accomplished theologians or even completely informed Christians by the time they enter the order of the faithful. All the faithful have an obligation to continue their learning and reflection on the truths of our faith and the workings of God in their lives. So, while the catechesis offered during this period should be complete enough for an intelligent initiation, it should also be recognized as only a beginning of ongoing catechesis.

The other part of that description of catechesis in the RCIA also deserves our careful consideration. The catechesis is to be gradual, the rite insists. This suggests that catechumens should be introduced to Catholic theology in a way that recognizes the varying importance of different doctrines. Some of the things we believe are central, while others are derivative or even peripheral. For example, while the Assumption of the Blessed Virgin Mary is important, it is clearly peripheral compared with the Incarnation of the Son of God. Focusing first on the central doctrines should flow rather naturally from basing the catechesis on the Scriptures, since our central beliefs are generally based more directly on the Bible than other, more derivative doctrines.

Even on a given topic, such as the Eucharist, there are many levels of theological explanation. What an inquirer can comprehend may well be less than what a catechumen can grasp, and a neophyte should be ready to explore the mystery of the

Eucharist even more fully after celebrating that sacrament. It may be valuable or even necessary to return to some topics several times as the catechumens increase the depth of their understanding and faith. To attempt to convey too much too quickly not only leads to confusion but also tends to present doctrines as unimportant to a person's life because they answer questions that the candidates have not yet raised.

That is one of the most important insights into good catechesis: Doctrines should be linked to the concrete lives of the learners. If we find that we cannot discover any "real life" application or implication of a given doctrine, then we should not attempt to teach it. Either we do not understand the doctrine properly or it is not important enough to warrant the effort. If we ask ourselves what difference a given doctrine makes—or should make—in our own lives, we will quickly discover which beliefs are really central to our own faith. While it may also be necessary at times to correct our own perspective in light of the larger Church's approach (if we have put some peripheral doctrine at the center of our own spirituality), ascertaining the value of a doctrine in our lives is a good place to start when preparing to share our beliefs with catechumens.

The second dimension of the catechumenate period is developing a familiarity with the Christian way of life. Because this sounds a bit vague, it is easy to overlook this dimension of the initiation process or to take it for granted. In one sense, it should occur naturally as catechumens interact with members of the parish community. And perhaps it will if we make sure that there is adequate interaction with the whole parish.

On the one hand, this reminds us of the importance of the witness and example of the members of the order of the faithful. The initiation of new members is truly the business of all the baptized. The rite itself mentions "the example and support of sponsors, godparents, and the entire Christian community" as helping the catechumens to learn to turn to God in prayer, bear witness to the faith, keep their hopes set on Christ, follow the inspiration of the Holy Spirit, and practice love of neighbor even at the cost of self-renunciation (no. 75.2). The spiritual journey of conversion involves a change of outlook and conduct, which is best learned and developed by association with a community that shares its outlook and way of life. Those who belong to the order of the faithful have a serious responsibility to share their faith with, and offer their support to, the catechumens in their midst.

On the other hand, recognizing the importance of this dimension of the catechumenate period can give us a crucial insight into what the whole catechumenate is about. Catechumens form an order in the Church, a distinct group of members of the Christian community. But their order is a liminal state, a transitional order, not meant to be permanent. While we should always have some catechumens in our midst, those who enter the order are expected to be in it for a limited time.

The only other order like this in the Church is the ancient order of penitents (see my book *Penance: The Once and Future Sacrament* [Collegeville, 1988] for further discussion of this order and its possible revival today).

It can be very helpful to view the catechumenate as a process of simply associating the catechumens with the ongoing life of the Church long enough that they "catch" the faith. They learn and grow by association with, and by the example of, the members of the community. Hence we should make sure that the catechumens are included as much as possible in everything that we do as a parish. From festivals to Bible studies, from parish council meetings to retreats, from social action to spiritual direction, from CCD classes to adult education, the catechumens should be invited, encouraged, and even expected to take part in the whole range of activities that make up parish life. They learn by doing, more than by studying, what the Church is and what Christian life entails.

A good case could even be made that involving the catechumens in the full life of the parish community should be the central thrust of a catechumenate, with special sessions of study and reflection on their experiences being secondary to such involvement. Those who would quickly protest that their parish doesn't offer enough in its ordinary ongoing life to give the catechumens proper formation should take a good hard look at their parish life. If such formation is not available to catechumens, then it is not being offered to the members of the order of the faithful either.

Here, as with many other issues, the Rite of Christian Initiation of Adults calls us to examine whether our life as Church is what it should be. All Christians are called to ongoing conversion. If a parish does not offer opportunities to foster such conversion in all its members, then it is not being the Church we are called to be. Conversely, to the extent that we are all living up to our identity as a converting people, associating catechumens with our way of life should be a powerful way of fostering conversion within them.

At least by the time of admission to the order of catechumens, the candidates are to have sponsors to accompany them on their journey. According to the introduction to the RCIA, sponsors are persons "who have known and assisted the candidates and stand as witnesses to the candidates' moral character, faith, and intention" (no. 10). While this seems to assume that the sponsor has known the catechumen before he or she even came to the Church, it is also possible that a sponsor could be assigned to the catechumen during the precatechumenate period; the sponsor could come to know the catechumen well enough before admission to the order of catechumens to be able to testify to his or her intention and worthiness to enter that order.

Much discussion has occurred over whether sponsors should be chosen by the candidate or selected by the catechumenate team. A mixture of both may best approach the ideal. Historically, the sponsor was generally the one who brought the candidate to the community and vouched for his or her worthiness. Often today there will be one person or another who has been very influential in the candidate's initial decision to investigate the Church, and in many cases such a person will be the ideal choice for sponsor. On the other hand, the sponsors have a very important role to play in the catechumenate, so those chosen as sponsors must be both willing and able to carry out that role. Being a sponsor demands a considerable commitment of time, and the person who has influenced a candidate is not always willing or able to devote the time required.

A sponsor should also be a guide to the life of the Church today for the catechumen. In this time of renewal we may find sometimes that the influential person is simply not up-to-date enough to properly guide the catechumen. If such a person were truly open and willing to accompany the catechumen on the journey of growth and learning, it might be possible that they could accompany each other on the journey. Still, since the sponsor is supposed to be a guide, it would be much better to have someone who is in tune with the Church's life and approach today.

Many parishes find that it is best to assign sponsors to the catechumens, taking into account the possibility of selecting someone who has had an influence on the candidate's decision to seek initiation if that person can properly fulfill the role. But filling the function of a sponsor is the most important criterion in the final choice.

The role of a sponsor is a multi-faceted one. The sponsor serves as a companion on the journey, in a sort of ''buddy system.'' He or she is a person the catechumen can lean on and look to for support. Often sponsors and catechumens form lasting friendships that last far beyond the duration of the RCIA.

The sponsor is also a guide on various points about Catholic life. The sponsor is not a catechist and does not bear responsibility for the basic instruction, but there are hundreds of small details of Catholic tradition and practice that may not be covered in the catechetical sessions. The sponsor may be asked a lot of questions about the "little things" that a catechumen may not bring up in the formal sessions—things such as why we genuflect when we enter the church building or how to enroll a child in the Catholic school. In addition, the sponsors should be able to help the catechumens learn to apply their faith in day-to-day situations at home, at work, or in leisure activities. For this reason some parishes try to match sponsors and catechumens by age and life situation as much as possible. A sponsor who is a father with several children, for example, can help a catechumen who is a father grapple with issues of parenting and sharing faith with children.

The sponsor also serves as a guide to parish life and helps the catechumen to meet and interact with other members of the parish community. The sponsor's role can be understood overall as a link between the catechumen and the larger community. Whatever the sponsor can do to facilitate that interaction is a great help to a real initiation into the Church, fostering a true sense of becoming part of the community and belonging there.

The sponsor, of course, also serves in a liturgical role for the various rituals of the RCIA. The rite makes provision for a distinction between sponsor and godparent. If these roles are separate, the sponsor accompanies the catechumen on the journey through the precatechumenate and the catechumenate period. The godparent then takes over at the election for the sacraments on the First Sunday of Lent and continues through the postbaptismal catechesis.

The godparent also accepts a permanent relationship with the neophyte, just as the godparents of infants do. The godparent, of course, may be the same person who served as sponsor. This is generally to be preferred, since the relationship built up over the months (or years) of the catechumenate provides a solid base and a rich resource for the periods of enlightenment and mystagogy. It should be noted clearly that there is no provision whatsoever in the Rite of Christian Initiation of Adults for a godparent who is simply honorary and is present just for the Easter sacraments. The godparent, even if distinct from the sponsor, must be an active participant in the conversion journey of the catechumen.

The third dimension of the catechumenate period is one of worship and prayer. Various liturgical rites take place in this period, including minor exorcisms, blessings, anointing with the oil of catechumens, and (optionally) the presentations of the Creed and the Lord's Prayer. The primary rituals for this period, however, are the celebrations of the Word of God. While some of these celebrations are arranged especially for the catechumens, they are also expected to take part in the liturgy of the Word at Mass each Sunday. In the latter instance, the catechumens are to be dismissed from the assembly before the liturgy of the Eucharist proper begins. They are not dismissed to the parking lot, but to their own assembly, where they continue to reflect on the Word of God they have heard and share their insights into how it affects their lives.

This dismissal needs to be understood correctly by both the catechumens and the community as a whole. It is not a gesture of rejection or a lack of hospitality; it is rather a recognition that the Eucharist can be fully celebrated only by the baptized and that the catechumens have their own needs, which can best be met in their own assembly after they have shared in the liturgy of the Word with the faithful. The shift from the dismissal to full participation in the Eucharist at Easter is a significant part of the experience of moving from the liminal period that is the catechumenate to the aggregation into the order of the faithful. Moreover, the dismissal is part of the witness that catechumens give to the community. Simply by leaving they remind the faithful of the privilege that is theirs because of their baptism. They remind us of the importance of the Eucharist and of the dignity of our baptism. That is part of the ministry that they offer to the larger Church.

The fourth dimension of the catechumenate period is sharing in the mission of the Church, both in spreading the Word of God and in serving others. This is, in a sense, a part of the second dimension, since the whole community should be engaged in this mission, and associating the catechumens with the community's life and activity should include apostolic activity. Its designation in the RCIA as a separate dimension of this period serves to indicate how important it is that the catechumens accept the responsibility for mission. Even though they are in a period of formation, catechumens are members of the Church and thus have responsibility for the Church's mission. It is a potent reminder to all Christians that membership in the Church requires mission of all of us.

The Rite of Election

When it is the common judgment of the pastor, the catechists, the sponsor, the catechumen, and the whole community of faith that the catechumen is ready for the celebration of the sacraments of initiation, the period of the catechumenate comes to a close and the catechumen enters the period of purification and enlightenment. The step between these two periods is called the rite of election. To elect is to choose, and the catechumens are chosen by the community of faith for admission to the sacraments. The rite also notes that the choice by the community is founded on election by God, since it is God who calls us to baptism and who brings about the conversion on which the Church's choice is based.

This rite is generally celebrated by the bishop at the cathedral or some other central church(es) in the diocese.

Since the Rite of Christian Initiation of Adults is strongly based in the local community of faith, this celebration with the bishop is one clear reminder that the catechumens are also entering a broader, universal Church. At the same time, this moment is of great importance to the parish community, so the bishops of the United States have provided an optional rite to be used in the parish community just prior to the rite of election with the bishop. The rite is called the Sending of the Catechumens for Election, and it offers an opportunity for the parish to express its approval of the catechumens and to send them to the bishop with the parish's support and love.

The rite of election is also known as the enrollment of names because the candidates inscribe their names in the Book of the Elect, which lists all those who have been chosen for initiation. This choice by the Church is a moment of high significance. If possible, the whole assembly of the faithful should be given a chance to affirm the decision of the catechumenate team during the ceremony itself. There is always the danger that such approval will become merely routine, an empty ritual. It should stand as a clear reminder that the whole community of the faithful shares responsibility for the initiation of new members. It also serves as a focus of the commitment by the faithful to offer support during the period of enlightenment that begins with the rite of election. This rite is normally celebrated on the First Sunday of Lent and calls both the catechumens and the faithful to enter into a time of prayer and spiritual growth in preparation for the celebration of the sacraments of initiation at the Easter Vigil.

This focus on the celebration of the sacraments also brings a change in the names used to describe catechumens and sponsors. The sponsors now become known as godparents, since they are preparing for that role at the Easter sacraments. If a godparent other than the sponsor is chosen, the new godparent takes over the responsibility beginning with the rite of election. The candidates, though still catechumens in the broad sense, are now more properly called "the elect," the chosen ones. Other names from the ancient catechumenate are also used in the rite: the *illuminandi*, "those who will be illumined or enlightened" by Christ in baptism, or the *competentes* ("co-petitioners"), those who are joined together in asking for the sacraments and the gift of the Holy Spirit. Such emphasis on terms may seem to be mere ritualism, but it can serve to emphasize the movement of the candidates through this step and into the new period of enlightenment.

The Period of Purification and Enlightenment

This period is quite different from the preceding catechumenate period, and that difference should be clearly noted. Coinciding with Lent, the period of purification and enlightenment is intended to be a time of prayer and spiritual preparation for the celebration of the sacraments at Easter. It is not a time for continuing the catechetical instruction of the candidates, which is likely to happen if the whole Rite of Christian Initiation of Adults is compressed into a nine-month period. It is intended to be a time of "retreat," an extended period of intense spiritual growth. Emphasis in this period should be more on prayer and reflection than on study and learning. It is a time for the elect to purify their minds and hearts as they examine their consciences and do penance. The enlightenment of this period is not one of learning about Christ so much as the experience of coming to know Christ through personal encounter in prayer.

This period of purification and enlightenment was actually the origin of Lent historically. Begun as a time of preparation for the candidates for baptism, this period also invited the rest of the community to join with the elect in prayer and penance. This was not only a means of support and prayer for the candidates but also a time to renew the commitment of the faithful to live out the meaning of their own baptism.

The Rite of Christian Initiation of Adults offers us the opportunity to truly revitalize Lent in our parishes. For this to happen, two things are required. The first is that the faithful at large must come to see Lent once again as a time of baptismal renewal. The baptismal focus of the season must be made as clear as possible. The very presence of the elect will be the most potent factor in making this clear, but it should also be emphasized in homilies, bulletins, and every other forum available. The sacrament of penance should be encouraged in this period precisely as a means of deepening or recovering the conversion of life that baptism celebrates. It should be clear to the faithful that Lent is leading to baptism for the elect and to the renewal of baptismal promises for the faithful at Easter.

The second requirement for revitalizing Lent is that the parish as a whole enter into the season as a time of retreat. It is not a time for business as usual, for the frantic round of meetings and activities that fill up most nights of the year in most parishes. It should be a time when the ordinary activities of the parish stop, or at least are carried on with a clear spiritual focus. This is a good time for a parish council retreat, for evenings of recollection for the various commissions and committees, for retreats and prayer services for youth, etc. Even the catechetical curricula for students in Catholic schools and CCD programs should be adjusted to make Lent a time to focus on conversion, baptism, and renewal. In short, Lent should be a time for the entire parish community to go on retreat along with the order of catechumens so that all will be spiritually prepared to celebrate the sacraments together at Easter.

More rituals take place during this period than during the other periods of the RCIA. This is the primary time when the conversion journey of the catechumens is shared with the whole community.

Following the rite of election on the First Sunday of Lent, the community celebrates the scrutinies on the Third, Fourth, and Fifth Sundays of Lent. The word "scrutiny" refers to the self-searching of the elect. These rites are designed to heal all that is weak and sinful in the hearts of the candidates and to strengthen all that is upright and good. They include prayers of exorcism and call for deep repentance. The scrutinies are based on the Gospels for these three Sundays in Cycle A of the Lectionary: the woman at the well, the man born blind, and the raising of Lazarus. If the scrutinies are used in Cycles B and C, the readings from Cycle A are still to be used for these Masses (nos. 143, 146).

Some people have reservations about the scrutinies because of their stress on sin and evil. This reflects a general discomfort in our society and in the Church today in dealing honestly and bluntly with the reality of evil in our lives and in our society. The RCIA calls us to confront the reality of sin with a robust honesty. We are sinners and we live in a sinful culture. To gloss over those realities for fear of offending the candidates or of being too negative is to do the catechumens a grave disservice. The call to conversion always involves both a turning away from sin and a turning to Christ. Both dimensions need to be properly emphasized and celebrated in the Rite of Christian Initiation of Adults.

Some of our discomfort with the scrutinies may flow also from a view of sin in our lives that is too limited. If we focus only on personal sins, especially sexual sins, it may seem that we are invading the candidates' privacy or embarrassing them in front of the community. Surely by the time they are chosen for the sacraments, they should have abandoned any gross immorality. Why, then, do we offer prayers of exorcism and call them to repent?

A better understanding of the scrutinies can be gained if we broaden our perspective on sin. The power of evil in our lives is much more pervasive and much more subtle than grossly immoral acts. Evil pervades our society in numerous ways, and it infiltrates our hearts and minds, and influences our lives in ways that are subtle but no less real than more obvious sins. Father Jim Dunning of the North American Forum on the Catechumenate has suggested that the scrutinies might well focus on the "isms" that pervade our society and our own hearts. Such issues as racism, sexism, consumerism, militarism, nationalism, privatism, and cynicism are all manifestations of the power of evil in our society, and they affect us all more than we like to admit.

Let us examine a few of these manifestations that may be most important for initiation into the Church. One of the most important attitudes that needs to be confronted in our society is the rampant privatism or individualism of our culture. We come from the frontier tradition that has emphasized individual rights and freedoms, sometimes to the exclusion of any concern for the community or society at large. Our songs and our images abound with individualism: "Don't fence me in"; "I need more elbow room"; "You're invading my space"; "I did it my way"; "Leave me alone"; "It's my life"; the Lone Ranger; the hero riding off into the sunset, etc.

While there is certainly some value in that stress on the dignity and rights of the individual, membership in the Church also requires a strong sense of community and commitment to the common good, even at the expense of self. Recent decades have seen so much emphasis on self-fulfillment that the Christian ideal of self-sacrifice is very alien to many people. This stress on the individual has already infiltrated the Church itself in devastating ways. Any pastor knows the frustration of trying to deal with people who come to prepare for a wedding or a baptism and demand that they get what they want, regardless of Church law, parish policy, or the greater good of the community. There is a sense abroad that the Church must give people whatever they demand and must never ask of them that they make any commitment or fulfill any requirements or follow any policies. Perhaps the root problem is often not exactly selfishness but a sense that the Church exists for the convenience of the individual, while the individual has no responsibility for the community.

This attitude is rife in our culture, affecting every social institution from schools to political entities, from social service agencies to employers. In political life we seem to be caught in a web of special interests, with almost no one willing to work together with others for the common good. In businesses and factories many workers work only for the money, with no sense of responsibility for the health and viability of the company or without any commitment to preserve the environment or promote the common good. Many persons are vehement in demanding their wishes, and just as vehement in rejecting any call to responsibility for others.

That such an attitude is incompatible with Christianity should be obvious; unfortunately, for many people it is not. Candidates for initiation should be clearly and frequently confronted with the contradiction between this attitude of our society and the gospel call to love and responsibility for others. God calls us and saves us precisely in the context of community. Throughout Scripture, when God calls individuals, they are called to enter into or to form community.

We are called to be part of the people of God, to form one Body of Christ, to be united in the Holy Spirit and to carry on the mission of Christ for the sake of the whole world. The scrutinies might well be a time to celebrate the growing liberation from the evil of privatism that keeps us from fully responding to God's call.

Closely linked to privatism is a subjectivism that pervades

our culture at the current time. In the name of pluralism, many have come to view truth and reality as purely subjective. Whatever I believe is right is right for me. If you see it differently, that's fine. There is no real truth, no right way to do things, no proper understanding of reality. Linked to this is a natural conclusion that one religion is just as good as any other. Such an attitude resists the whole idea of any authoritative teaching or any common standards of behavior.

While Christians certainly should respect the honest beliefs of others, this does not imply that there is no truth or standard of behavior that ought to be recognized and observed in society. Some things are morally wrong, even if some people think they are right. Christians must be willing to stand up for gospel values even when others do not share their views. And those who seek to join the Church must be willing to accept the basic principles and way of life of Christians. This does not exclude the possibility of informed dissent on particular issues, but such dissent is very different from the attitude that everything is subjective. That attitude must also be confronted in the course of the catechumenate.

A third example of an attitude that needs to be confronted is the nationalism or provincialism that focuses only on those people or concerns that are in our own backyard. Our nation has known several periods of isolationism in its history, but Catholics are called, even by the name Catholic (= universal), to a worldwide consciousness and concern. Sometimes the provincialism is even narrower, with people unwilling to care for the poor in their own cities, preferring to limit the focus of their concern to their own neighborhood or even to their own families. Such restrictions on our loving are clearly incompatible with a commitment to follow the One who gave his life for the salvation of the whole world. Christians are called to love all people, even their enemies. Love of enemies is a good touchstone of how much we love our God, and it is one of the more radical demands of the gospel. Catechumens and the whole community need to be challenged by that call.

Other issues are of obvious importance in a society marked by poverty and racism, by militarism and materialism, by cynicism and sexism. We have used as examples three issues that relate directly to the call to community because that may be the most important of all the issues a catechumenate must confront in our own time. A viable catechumenate requires a strong community into which candidates can be initiated. Yet the Catholic Church has lost much of the easy community it had in this country when it was an immigrant Church bound by language, culture, and social class, its members often living in "Catholic ghettoes."

Forming a community based simply on the gospel is harder, and it is a major challenge we face today. Unless we confront the attitudes that make real community impossible, both in catechumens and in the whole parish, we will never succeed in becoming the kind of community of love and service that the Church is supposed to be. Since the period of purification and enlightenment is the time when the conversion journey of the catechumens is shared most fully with the larger parish community, it seems that the scrutinies might well be adapted in such a way that these attitudes can be confronted and converted in all of us.

The other rituals proper to the period of purification and enlightenment are the presentations of the Creed and the Lord's Prayer. We noted earlier that these rites can be celebrated during the catechumenate period, but their normal place is in the period of purification and enlightenment. The Creed is presented sometime during the week following the first scrutiny, and the Lord's Prayer is presented after the third scrutiny. Both should be committed to memory by the elect so that they can profess the Creed before their baptism and join the community in the Lord's Prayer at the Easter Eucharist.

Some people might wonder if these presentations are simply antiquated rituals, since they seem to have originated in the period during which only the baptized were allowed to be present for the Creed and the Lord's Prayer at Mass. The candidates would thus never have heard them before and would have to be taught them and commit them to memory. It is certainly true that our situation today is different, for most people know the Lord's Prayer before they present themselves for initiation, and anyone who walks in off the street can attend our Eucharist. Moreover, the Creed and the Lord's Prayer can easily be found in print today, which was not a possibility in the third or fourth century.

Nevertheless, these ritual presentations can still serve a valuable function if they are seen as a time to stress the importance of these formulas and to entrust them to the elect as their own. The Creed is a summary of our faith, and the Lord's Prayer is the model for all our praying. These two formulas, then, serve as "hooks" on which the rest of our belief and prayer can be hung. A formal presentation of these texts, perhaps beautifully inscribed on vellum or parchment, perhaps slowly and carefully recited, can be seen as an important gift from the church community to the elect.

The period of purification and enlightenment comes to a conclusion with the paschal fast of Good Friday and Holy Saturday. The whole Church is encouraged to continue the fast of Good Friday until the celebration of the Easter Vigil. The elect are advised to refrain from their usual activities on Saturday and to spend the day in prayer, reflection, and fasting. If it is possible to bring the candidates together for joint prayer, several rites may be used: the recitation or "giving back" of the Creed, the presentation of the Lord's Prayer (if it has not been celebrated earlier), the ephphetha rite, and the choosing of a baptismal name.

Celebration of the Sacraments of Initiation

The third step of the Rite of Christian Initiation of Adults is the celebration of the initiation sacraments at the Easter Vigil. This is the culmination of the whole process, celebrated in the context of the only liturgy of the year with enough splendor and richness to sustain the meaning of this event. The rite notes that if the initiation process is being carried out at some other time of the year due to extraordinary circumstances, care must be taken that the celebration of the sacraments has "a markedly paschal character" (no. 208).

It is important to realize here that the celebration of these initiation sacraments is the core of the whole Easter celebration. Too often we think of Easter as just a commemoration of an event that occurred almost two thousand years ago. The resurrection we celebrate is not just a past historical event but the rising of Christ here today in these candidates who are baptized into new life. It is in them that Christ conquers death and rises to new life, and it is their (and our) sharing in that new life which we celebrate at Easter.

The celebration of baptism can be done in one of three ways: by immersion of the whole body, by immersion of the head only, or by pouring water over the candidate's head. Obviously, the physical design of the baptistry or a temporary font may limit the possibility of full immersion, but parishes should not dismiss this option too quickly. Because it conveys most fully the significance of being buried with Christ and rising to new life in him, full immersion should be considered the preferred method of baptism. When church buildings are designed or remodeled, the possibility of font designs that allow for immersion should be considered. Where such major changes are not feasible, it is often possible to arrange a temporary font in the sanctuary for immersion at the Easter Vigil. Proper decorum should be observed, of course, but the richness of the symbol adds significantly to the celebration of baptism.

We noted earlier the strong insistence of the RCIA that adults are not to be baptized without receiving confirmation immediately afterward. The rite bases this insistence on "the unity of the paschal mystery, the close link between the mission of the Son and the outpouring of the Holy Spirit, and the connection between the two sacraments through which the Son and the Holy Spirit come with the Father to those who are baptized" (no. 215). As Aidan Kavanagh noted years ago, Rome does not invoke the Trinity for mere rhetoric. The paragraph just cited is a heavy theological statement about the meaning of confirmation and its intimate link with baptism. While one might legitimately wonder why confirmation is still separated from baptism in the initiation of children, there is no doubt that the RCIA expects the integral celebration of the sacraments of initiation to be the norm.

Following their baptism and confirmation, the neophytes join the rest of the faithful in the celebration of the Easter Eucharist. No longer catechumens, they are now members of the order of the faithful, and as such they properly take key roles in the general intercessions (prayer of the faithful) and the presentation of the gifts. Praying the Lord's Prayer for the first time as members of the faithful, they express their adoption as children of God. Sharing in the sacred meal of the body and blood of the Lord, they are strengthened in their conversion and given a foretaste of the eternal banquet in which they will share in heaven.

The Period of Postbaptismal Catechesis or Mystagogy

The final period of the Rite of Christian Initiation of Adults is called "mystagogy." This ancient term means the study of the mysteries and refers to the kind of catechesis that is possible only after the sacraments have been experienced. While it is likely that the sacraments had not even been explained before this period in the ancient catechumenate, it is still important today to have the opportunity to probe the richness of these "mysteries" (the ancient term for the sacraments) in light of the experience of celebrating them at Easter. That is the catechesis which is expected in this fourth period of the RCIA.

The emphasis in this period is on the interaction between the neophytes (the newly baptized) and the rest of the faithful. The benefits flow in both directions. The neophytes should experience a warm sense of welcome into the order of the faithful and develop closer ties with other members of that order. At the same time, the rest of the faithful should derive a fresh sense of inspiration and a renewed outlook from their association with those whose experience of the Lord is so fresh.

Since this period focuses on the experience of the sacraments and the community of the faithful, the postbaptismal catechesis is carried out primarily in the context of the Sunday Eucharist in the midst of the community. The readings of the Lectionary for the Sundays of the Easter season, especially in Cycle A, are particularly suited for exploring the meaning of the initiation sacraments and the living out of that meaning in daily Christian life.

The period of mystagogy is also a time for the neophytes to be integrated more fully into the ongoing life and activities of the faithful. As members of that order, they now take on full responsibility for the ongoing mission of the Church in the world. With the example and support of the other members of their new order, they begin to put into practice the implications of the sacraments they have celebrated.

This period concludes with a celebration held on or near Pentecost, but the national statutes for the United States call for at least monthly assemblies of the neophytes throughout the first year after their initiation. This national statute flows from the experience of neophytes in our country—they have often noted that the end of the regular meetings they experienced in the catechumenate leaves them a bit lost. There is a real need for an ongoing experience of community in a group smaller than most parishes provide. These monthly meetings can do much to help the neophytes to continue their spiritual growth and to be fully integrated into the order of the faithful.

At the end of that year there is to be an anniversary celebration in which the neophytes can give thanks to God, share their spiritual experiences, and renew their commitment (no. 250). Sometime in the course of that year the bishop, if he did not personally preside at the sacraments of initiation, should meet the newly baptized and preside at a celebration of the Eucharist with them.

QUESTIONS FOR REFLECTION

1. Do you find it more helpful to view the RCIA as a process articulated by rituals or as a series of rituals and the preparation leading to them?

2. Which period of the RCIA seems most challenging for your parish to implement well?

3. What will it take for your parish to become an evangelizing community of faith?

4. How can we make it clear that admission to the catechumenate is truly acceptance into the Church, that catechumens are really members of the Church?

5. Does the approach to catechesis in the RCIA seem like a major shift to you? Does a catechesis that is gradual, complete, and tied to the liturgical year make sense to you?

6. How can you introduce catechumens to all the dimensions of Christian life in your parish? Could this be the main thrust of a catechumenate in your parish? Does your parish offer enough opportunities for growth for all its members?

7. How do you think sponsors should be chosen for catechumens and candidates for full communion with the Church?

8. How important should the role of the bishop be throughout the RCIA? How involved is the bishop in your diocese?

9. How can we make the period of purification and enlightenment a time of intense spiritual growth for catechumens? for the whole parish?

10. Is your parish comfortable talking about and confronting evil? with catechumens? in the parish? in our society?

11. How can we combat the extreme individualism of our culture and develop a stronger sense of a community of faith?

12. How central is the Easter Vigil in your parish? How can we help our communities really celebrate the Vigil?

13. How should the period of mystagogy differ from the other periods of the RCIA? How can we involve the whole parish in this period of reflection on our risen life in Christ?

CHAPTER SIX

ADAPT, ADAPT, ADAPT

Thus far we have been talking about the initiation of unbaptized adults, which is obviously the main focus of the Rite of Christian Initiation of Adults. The normal pastoral situation in the United States, however, presents us with a number of variations on that theme. We have many adults coming for initiation who have already been baptized in another Christian denomination. Among them are some who were very active and educated in their own Church and others who were never more than nominal members. We also see adults who were baptized as Catholics but were never raised in the faith. Some persons coming for re-initiation have been away from the Church for many years. We have teenagers who want to convert on their own, sometimes in spite of family opposition. And we have children of various ages who need to be initiated, either because their Catholic parents neglected to have them baptized as infants or because their parents are being initiated into the Catholic Church and want their children to share their new faith. These and many other variations occur with confusing regularity in most parishes of any significant size.

The complexity of trying to provide for such a range of needs and expectations can be overwhelming at times, but it is inherent in the initiation arena. Initiation involves unique, individual faith journeys at the same time as it involves a community experience and ritual articulation. Thus there is always going to be some tension between the needs of the individuals involved and the normative character of the process of initiation into the community.

It is for that reason that the RCIA has more provisions for adaptation than any of the other revised rites issued since the Second Vatican Council. These adaptations are made on various levels, from the National Conference of Catholic Bishops, to a local diocese, to the local parish. Some adaptations have been made on a national level by our bishops and are contained in the additional rites and the national statutes included in the current editions of the RCIA. These national adaptations resulted from the experiences of parishes across the country since the RCIA was issued in its provisional translation in 1974.

Catechumens and Candidates for Full Communion

One of the most obvious differences between the situation in the United States and that of many other countries is the pluralism of Christian denominations here. Hence, one of the most basic adaptations needed in this country involves the process of initiation for those already baptized in another denomination. Most parishes have found it impractical thus far to run entirely separate programs for the true catechumens (the unbaptized) and for those already baptized.

Since many of those coming to join the Catholic Church from another Christian Church need much of the same instruction and formation as the unbaptized do, it makes sense in many circumstances to combine both groups.

It is absolutely essential, however, that we do not suggest that we are rebaptizing or that the baptism of other Christian Churches is invalid. The baptized are in a significantly different situation than the unbaptized. The bishops therefore insist that those already baptized should never be called "catechumens" or "converts." They are baptized Christians preparing to be received into full communion with the Catholic Church. A clear distinction should always be made between these two groups throughout the initiation process.

Since both groups travel a similar journey, however, it often makes sense to have them celebrate that journey together ritually. For this purpose the adaptations for the United States provide several combined rites (see Appendix I) for (a) acceptance into the order of catechumens and welcoming baptized adults preparing for confirmation and/or Eucharist or reception into full communion; (b) sending catechumens for election and candidates for recognition by the bishop; (c) the rite of election of catechumens and the call to continuing conversion of candidates preparing for confirmation and/or Eucharist or reception into full communion with the Catholic Church; and (d) the Easter Vigil celebration of the sacraments of initiation and of the rite of reception into the full communion of the Catholic Church. The very titles of these combined rites (actually abbreviated here!) indicate the complexity of the groups that many parishes experience. The bishops have also provided a series of rituals not included in the Roman typical edition for the preparation of uncatechized adults for confirmation and Eucharist (chapter 4). These can be used with those who were baptized as Catholics but not catechized or with those baptized in another denomination.

The list of combined rites includes a rite for sending the catechumens and the candidates to the bishop. The basic rite of sending catechumens to the bishop, we noted earlier, is also an American adaptation. Many parishes began using the Rite of Christian Initiation of Adults before their bishops or dioceses began to take it seriously and thus became accustomed to celebrating the rite of election in the parish. As a very significant step in the process of initiation, this had great impact on their parish communities. As bishops began to take more interest and become involved in the RCIA, they began to celebrate the rite of election in the cathedral or some other central location. The void that was created in the local parish when the rite of election "moved downtown" led to the creation of a rite for sending the catechumens (and candidates) from the local community to the bishop. This rite provides an opportunity for the parish to celebrate the progress of the catechumens and candidates and still maintains the role of the bishop in the initiation process; it also reminds the initiates that they are joining a Church that is much larger than the local parish.

The process of formation that these various rites celebrate must be tailored to the needs of those who come for initiation. A well-educated and active Episcopalian who comes seeking full communion in the Catholic Church would not likely need a full catechumenal process, for example. Chapter 5 of the Rite of Christian Initiation of Adults is titled "Reception of Baptized Christians into the Full Communion of the Catholic Church."

The simplicity of the rite described here should be understood carefully. On the one hand, it reminds us that some people who are just "changing Christian denominations" may not need intensive conversion therapy. We should not rashly assume that everyone who seeks full communion has the same needs as a catechumen.

On the other hand, the introduction to chapter 5 clearly indicates that such candidates should receive appropriate "doctrinal and spiritual preparation" for reception (no. 477), and the American adaptations for chapter 4 provide a whole series of rituals that can be used to celebrate the stages of their progress.

The Initiation of Children of Catechetical Age

The other major area that requires adaptation in the RCIA is the Christian initiation of children who have reached catechetical age. That age is not precisely defined, but the rite speaks of those who "have attained the use of reason and are of catechetical age" (no. 252). This seems to suggest that even young children in the primary grades are to be initiated with this rite. Obviously we should not expect an adult conversion from them, but the rite calls for a conversion that is "personal and somewhat developed, in proportion to their age" (no. 253). It also notes that their initiation may be extended over several years, if need be, as with adults.

The initiation of children should be carried on and celebrated as much as possible in a community of their peers, and the rite suggests that their celebration of the sacraments be linked closely to the time at which their peers receive confirmation or Eucharist. At the same time, the rite calls for the celebration of the sacraments at the Easter Vigil and presumes the integral celebration of all three sacraments of initiation (no. 305). Since their peers who were baptized as infants do not generally receive confirmation and Eucharist at the same time, it seems that these provisions are designed to link the full sacramental initiation of these children with the same general time period that their peers would be celebrating Eucharist *or* confirmation, depending on the age of the initiates.

The rite makes no provision for baptizing and giving first Eucharist to such a child while reserving confirmation to a later age. All three sacraments are always to be celebrated together in the traditional order, whether the catechumens are adults or children of catechetical age. Even children baptized in another denomination should celebrate confirmation and Eucharist in the same ceremony (no. 308).

Other Adaptations

Two other rites are provided for exceptional situations in chapters 2 and 3. In individual cases the bishop may permit a simpler form of Christian initiation to be used in place of the usual, complete rite. This rite (chapter 2) is provided for cases in which some circumstance prevents the candidate from completing the full catechumenate or when the candidate has such a depth of conversion and religious maturity that the bishop decides baptism should be celebrated without delay. Chapter 3 provides a rite of Christian initiation for a person in danger of death and is a brief emergency rite that includes baptism, confirmation, and viaticum.

Beyond the adaptations that have been made by the nation's bishops, other decisions may be made by the local bishop. But much of the adaptation of the Rite of Christian Initiation of Adults must be made in the local situation, both in terms of deciding which adaptations apply to which candidates and in terms of further adaptation of the wording of prayers and use of the options in the various rites. The key in this local adaptation is finding a balance between the desire to tailor the process to local and individual needs and the necessity of keeping the process standard enough that it is recognizable as initiation into the Roman Catholic Church.

The elements that are part of the RCIA are all there for good reasons. Any adaptation of the rite must be made with a clear understanding of those reasons, and the goals of the original process must be maintained in any adapted process or ritual. The Rite of Christian Initiation of Adults makes great demands on our parish communities. Much of its value will be lost if it is toned down and modified simply for convenience or to make initiation easier somehow. It needs to be implemented in its robust fullness if it is to help us become once again an initiating assembly of God's holy people.

QUESTIONS FOR REFLECTION

1. What percentage of inquirers in your parish are unbaptized? Does this indicate anything about how evangelization occurs in your area?

2. What adaptations do you feel are necessary in implementing the RCIA in your parish?

3. How can your parish keep clear the distinction between catechumens and candidates for full communion throughout the initiation process?

4. Has your parish developed an adaptation of the RCIA for children? If not, what will it take to do so?

5. What circumstances can you envision that would warrant using the exceptional forms of initiation in chapters 2 and 3 of the RCIA?

6. Are there other adaptations that you think our bishops should have made in the RCIA? Why?

CHAPTER SEVEN

TRY TO REMEMBER

We began this book speaking about a puzzle, a new puzzle that requires new pieces if the picture is to come out right. In the course of the book we have looked at a whole collection of new pieces that make up the puzzle of a Church renewed as an initiating assembly. In this final chapter we would like to briefly recall some of those pieces, some of the most important things to remember about the Rite of Christian Initiation of Adults. These are issues that need to be kept in mind throughout the planning and carrying out of the RCIA, issues that need much reflection and sharing by a catechumenate staff as well as probing with other parishes and diocesan leaders. They are some of the key pieces that will help us work on the right puzzle.

Puzzle Piece #1: *Remember that the Rite of Christian Initiation of Adults is not a program through which we put people.* Many writers insist that it is not a program but a process. The latter term is not entirely suitable either, because it can still imply that people are being "processed" through our system. What the RCIA requires is the reestablishment of an order in the Church—the order of catechumens. Like any other order in the Church, this order will include persons with different rates of growth and with different styles of spirituality. The order does call for some uniformity (remember the liminal period), but it also makes room for the uniqueness of each person's response to the Lord's call to conversion. We have spoken at length of the process that must underlie the celebration of the rituals, of the conversion that catechumens must experience before it makes sense to celebrate together. But the process of conversion is somewhat unique to each person, and it is each person's lived experience of God that is brought to a common celebration of God's saving grace.

Puzzle Piece #2: *Remember that catechesis is more than instruction.* The Rite of Christian Initiation of Adults will likely have a profound effect over time on how we understand catechesis in the Church, not only for catechumens but for all members of the community. For too long catechesis has been divorced from the rest of the community's life. The RCIA reminds us that catechesis should be based on the Sunday Lectionary, so that it flows from the proclamation of the Word of God in Scripture. Catechesis should be clearly linked to the liturgical year as a result of its connection with our Sunday worship. The RCIA also reminds us that the goal of all catechesis is conversion, so it must respect the dynamics of conversion and spiritual growth in individuals. And finally the RCIA reminds us that catechesis must be linked to daily living, integrating moral awareness with prayer and doctrinal learning. Good catechesis is always linked to the actual experience of God that people have in their lives. Catechesis helps people to name and interpret their experience so that they learn to recognize God's presence and action and promptings in their own lives. Some of this has already been realized by many religious educators, but we have a long way to go before it is incarnated in the way we do catechesis in most parishes.

Puzzle Piece #3: *Remember that the Rite of Christian Initiation of Adults requires a multitude of different ministries.* In the not too distant past, the responsibility for the instruction

of converts usually rested on the shoulders of one person—
the pastor or an associate pastor. He was the one who wel-
comed the inquirer, gave the instructions, conducted a tour
of the church building, judged the candidate's readiness, in
some cases chose the godparent, conducted the baptism
(usually on a Saturday afternoon when nobody was looking!),
and recorded the information in the parish record book.

The pattern envisioned by the Rite of Christian Initiation
of Adults is quite different. The rite lists sponsors, godparents,
the bishop, priests, deacons, and catechists, along with the
whole community of the faithful, as those who have official
ministries in the RCIA. In addition, many parishes have developed other specific roles as part of the catechumenate team,
such as ministers of hospitality, liturgy coordinators for the
various rituals, spiritual directors, retreat leaders, sponsor coordinators, facilitators for the dismissal sessions during Sunday Mass, prayer leaders, recruiters and evangelizers. The
importance of this expansion of ministries is not that it relieves
the priest of a great burden but that the catechumenate models
an image of the Church. Just as the Church is larger and more
varied than the priest, so the model presented by the catechumenate team should be as broad as possible to reflect the
diversity of perspectives and talents needed in the Church.
Even in formal catechesis, it is valuable if the catechumens have
a variety of catechists so that more than one person's view-
point is presented for consideration.

Puzzle Piece #4: *Remember that the initiation of new mem-*
bers is the business of all the baptized. This piece is a corollary
to the previous one. The largest group of ministers who are
to be involved in the catechumenate is also the easiest one to
overlook. The whole order of the faithful has a serious responsibility to welcome and support those who seek initiation into
their order. As long as this task is left to priests and other ''pro-

fessional religious'' people, the Church will not be the lay-centered community that the Second Vatican Council has called us to be.

It is the faithful who must evangelize their families, friends, neighbors, and co-workers. It is they who must invite people to investigate and examine the Catholic Church to see if that is where God is calling them. It is the faithful who must create an atmosphere of hospitality and concern that will both draw people to the Church and encourage them to stay once they have come. It is the faithful who must witness by their daily lives to what the Christian life means, both to attract non-believers to Christ and to help inquirers understand what conversion requires of them. It is the faithful who must offer support and encouragement to the catechumens in their midst, sometimes serving as sponsors for them. It is the baptized who must join in prayer and fasting and celebration both for and with the candidates for initiation. It is the faithful who must gather for the Easter Vigil as the most important liturgy of the year and make the celebration of Easter come alive. It is the baptized who must make the initiation of new members the center of the parish's life, accepting the mission Christ has given us. It is the faithful who will ultimately determine whether a parish is an initiating assembly or not.

A major challenge for the catechumenate team, therefore, is to find creative ways to involve all members of the parish in the initiation process. Constant communication with the parish through the bulletin and from the pulpit is essential. Various parish groups and organizations should be invited to take responsibility for different aspects of the catechumenate and to offer support for particular catechumens. School and CCD children can be linked with individual catechumens, especially those students preparing for confirmation or first Eucharist themselves. Shut-ins can be asked to pray for those being initiated. Prayer groups and Bible study groups can be invited to share their experiences with the catechumens as part of their formation. In these and dozens of other ways, the various members of the order of the faithful can be brought into the experience of initiation of new members.

Puzzle Piece #5: *Remember that the Rite of Christian Initiation of Adults redefines what it means to be a Christian and what it means to be the Church.* Father Aidan Kavanagh hazarded a guess in 1974 that when historians look back at our era, they will see the RCIA as the single most important result of Vatican II. He said this not because of its ritual changes but because of the robust vision of the Church contained in the rite. This puzzle piece is closely related to the previous two, for the sense of the Church as a community of ministers is central to the vision of Church implied in the RCIA. Perhaps especially in this country, because we were for so long an immigrant Church whose time was taken up with caring for our own, we have not had a very vital sense of being the Church for the sake of others, for the salvation of the world. We need to recover a sense of the mission of the Church, to recognize that God has called us to be instruments for the salvation of others. The most important question the Gospel asks us is not whether we are saved but whether God can use us to save others.

The Rite of Christian Initiation of Adults presents a vision of a Church that is a caring faith community, a Church that reaches out to others with the Good News of Jesus Christ, a Church constantly living in the Spirit and discerning the action of that Spirit of God, a Church whose life revolves around the initiation of new members and the continual conversion of all its members. It is a Church that is not self-centered but salt for the earth and light for the world.

While it is true that any vision of the Church is somewhat idealistic, the vision presented in the RCIA is a solid ideal to-

ward which to strive. It may also be a quite different image
of the Church than many of our parishioners have, a quite
different Church than we have known in the concrete reality
of our parishes. It is perhaps this reason more than any other
that has kept many parishes from taking the Rite of Christian
Initiation of Adults seriously over the past fifteen years. To embrace the RCIA is to commit ourselves to a radical renewal of
our life as the Church. It is no small challenge!

Puzzle Piece #6: *Remember that the catechumenate is a place
for serious theology, not a watered-down Sunday school.*
Remember that it was in the classical catechumenate that much
of the best theology of the early centuries of the Church developed. The catechumenate is the place where the gospel and
the culture meet and interact. Out of that interaction will come
the theology of our own time. It is interesting to note that the
most fertile field of theology in recent years has been liberation theology. That theology has developed to a significant degree from small Christian communities meeting to discuss the
gospel and apply it to their daily social situations. It is the same
kind of reflection and catechesis that is required in the
catechumenate, and it should lead us to a theology that is always developing, addressing new issues in our culture and
society as they arise and affect our lives.

I do not mean to suggest that all catechumens must become
professional theologians. But theology is simply an attempt to
understand the revelation of God in our own time and its implications for our daily lives. It is that kind of grass-roots theology that is needed to enable the Church to be the salt of the
earth and the leaven in the dough. It is only to the extent that
the gospel is applied to the real issues of people's lives that
the Church will be the agent of transforming the world that
we are called to be. It is that kind of reading the signs of the

times and applying gospel insights to daily life that we must teach catechumens to do.

This kind of interaction between gospel and culture can be threatening to those who think they already have all the answers. While there is a necessity to convey the long and developed tradition of the Church to candidates for initiation, it is also important to provide enough freedom for the candidates to truly probe the meaning of their lives in light of the gospel and to probe the meaning of the gospel in light of their life experience. Some have suggested that to ensure this kind of freedom to think and question, the priest should not be part of the catechumenate sessions. There may be some merit to this suggestion if the priest is rather authoritarian in style or if the particular candidates seem highly intimidated by the clergy. But the involvement of the pastor in an open and probing discussion can also go a long way toward overcoming such intimidation and can present a much healthier view of both clergy and Church. Often a balance can be achieved by having the pastor present regularly but not for every session. What is most important, though, is the attitude taken by the pastor whenever he is there. An open and questioning approach can be much more helpful than a closed attitude that claims to have all the answers.

Puzzle Piece #7: *Remember that the role of sponsor is crucial to the catechumenate experience.* Evaluations we have done with different groups of neophytes have indicated that the sponsors were frequently viewed as the single most helpful part of their experience of initiation. In the personal relationship that can and should develop between catechumen and sponsor, there is a great potential for both support and influence during the catechumenate.

Sponsors should be chosen with care and given adequate formation in understanding the role before they accept the responsibility. Throughout the catechumenate, sponsors should be given support in fulfilling their role and should be carefully heard when they make suggestions or raise questions that have come from their interaction with the catechumens or candidates. Sponsors should be part of the catechumenate team and should be fully informed of what is happening in the process and what is expected of them. Some parishes insist that sponsors attend all sessions with the candidates; others feel that sponsors who are heavily involved in other areas of parish life should not be compelled to make such a time commitment. Whatever decision is made on that issue, good communication with sponsors is essential to a good catechumenate.

Puzzle Piece #8: *Remember that the Rite of Christian Initiation of Adults will raise numerous questions about many aspects of parish life.* These questions will generally be both threatening and important. They must be faced honestly, and the need for change in how we live out the gospel as a parish should be recognized and accepted. Some of these questions have been hinted at earlier, especially in the area of catechesis. The following are the kinds of questions the RCIA will and should raise for us.

Why do we have Catholic schools and CCD programs? Is their goal conversion? How do they achieve it? Do they? How can we change them to promote real conversion? Are our catechetical programs linked to the liturgical year?

When do we celebrate initiation sacraments and why do we pick those days? When is first penance celebrated and why? Does penance really belong before first communion? What does first communion have to do with Mother's Day? When is confirmation celebrated? Shouldn't it be between baptism and first Eucharist? Should all three initiation sacraments always be celebrated together? At what age? Why?

What does it mean to be a member of the order of the faithful? How do the orders of deacons, priests, and bishops relate to the order of the faithful? Which order in the Church is really central? How does the reestablishment of the order of catechumens redefine the other orders? Do we also need an order of penitents for those Catholics who feel a need for a catechumenal-type experience to deepen their own conversion?

What does the Rite of Christian Initiation of Adults teach us about the initiation of infants? Should we continue to baptize infants? Why or why not? If we baptize them, should we also confirm them and give them the Eucharist? Why or why not? What is really required for confirmation? Does it make sense to require more for confirmation than for baptism? What is confirmation anyway? What does celebrating that sacrament mean? Does it make sense to celebrate it separately from baptism?

What does it mean to celebrate any sacrament? What is the underlying process that each sacrament articulates? Who are sacraments for—the "recipients" or the community? Who celebrates a marriage—just the couple or the whole assembly? Should sacraments ever be celebrated privately? Should sacraments ever be "family-only" affairs?

What is the meaning of Lent in our parish? How do we observe it? How do we keep Easter for fifty days? Why is the Eucharist more popular during Lent than during Easter? Why do so few people come to celebrate the Easter Vigil? Do we know how to celebrate our faith?

How supportive are we as a community? How welcoming are we? How can we learn to speak more freely and openly of our faith? How can we learn to be an evangelizing community? What is the purpose of our parish life? How do those outside our faith community see us? Is our mission clear to them? To us? What does it mean to be the Church? Do we provide a healthy community life for neophytes after their initiation?

Is it obvious to every member of our parish that to be a Christian is to be a servant and to carry on the mission of Christ in the world?

The questions go on and on, for the Rite of Christian Initiation of Adults challenges almost every aspect of our parish life. The questions will make us uneasy, for they call us to conversion as a community. That will mean a letting go of our past and a willingness to change and grow in Christ, and such change is always painful before it brings joy. We must face the questions and grapple with them if we are to be alive in Christ. That is the promise and the challenge of the RCIA.

Puzzle Piece #9: *Remember that the purpose of a catechumenate is not to get everyone into the Church.* This issue is one of evaluation. How do we determine when we have a "successful" catechumenate? What does success mean in this realm? If one or several of our candidates decide not to join the Church, is that a sign of failure on our part? If we start with that assumption, we will be continually tempted to water down the RCIA so that it entails no hard demands or difficult decisions. The result would be shallow conversions or no conversions.

The work of conversion is ultimately God's work and we cannot judge our efforts by the number we convince to join. Our task is to facilitate the work of the Holy Spirit. It may be that God is not really calling some of our inquirers to join the Church. It may be that God's call is to join at some later time. It may be that God is calling, but the inquirer is not ready to answer that call yet. The responsibility of the Church is to test the validity of the call (discern the Spirit's action) and then support the candidate through the conversion experience as God brings it about.

I believe that God calls to baptism and membership in the Church those who are to be the light, the salt, and the leaven for the world. Those Gospel images should remind us that the Church is not identified with the whole world but is called to be an agent of change within the world and servant to the world. We have a mission to carry out, and only those who are ready to take on that mission are ready for initiation into the Church.

Puzzle Piece #10: *Remember that it is God who brings about conversion both in catechumens and in us.* This is a corollary to the previous piece, of course, but it cannot be emphasized too much that we are not ultimately in charge of conversion. God's activity is primary and our efforts are always secondary. We are God's servants, and we try to be faithful to that service. We are instruments that God can use to carry on the work of Christ in the world. But we can only be good instruments if we remember our place and allow God to have God's way with us.

The ministry of fostering conversion in catechumens and candidates requires a constant willingness to undergo conversion in our own lives. The more we turn ourselves over to God and let God be in charge of our lives and our ministry, the more effective our efforts will be, because we will learn to stay out of God's way and let the Spirit work. So often we place obstacles in the way of God's grace, and we can help others remove the obstacles in their lives only to the extent that we become open channels through which God's grace can flow. We must often remove the plank in our own eye before we can see to remove the speck in our neighbor's eye.

Thus, the Rite of Christian Initiation of Adults calls each of us to a deeper conversion, to a constant conversion, to a fuller conversion. The more I work with catechumens, the more I am convinced that I gain more than I give to them. It is hard to come that close to the fire of the Holy Spirit without being warmed and cheered by that fire. Sometimes it sears a little, too, but that only burns away the parts of me that are dead and need to be pruned that I might come to fuller life. May the Lord lead us all into the fullness of life and joy which Christ came to bring us!

QUESTIONS FOR REFLECTION

1. Which of the ten puzzle pieces will be hardest for you to remember? Why?

2. With how many of these pieces is your parish already working? Which ones are nowhere in sight yet?

3. What is the next puzzle piece you should try to put in place?

4. Can you begin to see the shape of the picture on this new puzzle? How do you react to that picture of the Church? Does it excite you or frighten you or both?

5. What effects has the RCIA already had on other areas of your parish life? What else needs to change in your parish?

6. Which of these pieces would be the most fruitful as a focus for your own reflection and prayer?

7. Do you think Aidan Kavanagh is correct when he suggests that the RCIA is the most important result of Vatican II? Why or why not?